Arkansas State Parks

Travel to all the State Parks in Arkansas.

This book belongs to _____

Call this number if found _____

My Nature Book Adventures

arkansasstateparks.com/parks/map

mynaturebookadventures.com

Adventure Begins

The **ARKANSAS** State Parks Adventure Book is part planner, part journal, and 100% your adventure! Created to include dedicated space for you to plan your journey and share your experience. Check out each of the Parks and cross them off your MUST DO exploration list. Then look back at the experiences with your family and friends. Plan your adventures, then share all of the fun! Decorate your pages YOUR way.

Find your next adventure and share your treasured memories!

We have organized each park in alphabetical order, making it easy to find the park you are looking for. Each map has a pin to match the location of the destination to be used with the table of contents, identifying the page number you can find each location. Use the table of contents as your KEY to the map inside.

Spend your time surrounded in nature, taking in all of the unique geological features, and unusual ecosystems within the ARKANSAS State Parks. Write about the special moments from each destination inside. You are creating your own special keepsake and making cherished lifelong memories. So what are you waiting for. It's time to explore!

GROTTO FALLS - PETIT JEAN STATE PARK

Inside your book you will find...

ON THE LEFT SIDE OF EACH 2 PAGE SPREAD, YOU HAVE

A place to plan the details of your trip.

A would you return area

A section for reservation information, including refund policy, reserved dates, address, check-in and check-out times, website, phone, wifi information, and even a place for your confirmation number.

Plus an area to show how far you are traveling.

A fun color-in of the transportation modes you used during your adventures in the park.

A space to attach your favorite postcard, picture, drawing, stamp and ticket stub.

THE RIGHT SIDE INCLUDES PARK INFORMATION AND GIVES YOU A PLACE TO SHARE THE SPECIAL MOMENTS ABOUT YOUR JOURNEY

Park Information

The county the park is located in

The year the park was established

The location and contact information of the park

Special Moments

Include why you went

Who went with you

When you went

What you did

The souvenir you brought home

What you saw

What you learned

An unforgettable moment

A laughable moment

A surprising moment

A unforgettable moment

An unforeseeable moment

A QR code for the most up to date park information available

A fun color-in of the weather you experienced during your adventures

Make it all about YOU and your journey!

Also inside is an adventure checklist to make your adventures even more memorable.

We want you to spend every moment of your trip enjoying every bit of the ARKANSAS State Parks!

ADVENTURE

What you will find at the parks...

Buffalo River

Website: https://www.arkansasstateparks.com/

TABLE OF CONTENTS

Let THE adventure BEGIN

· ADVENTURE IS CALLING ·

EXPLORE

What you will find at the parks...

Mt Magazine

Website: https://www.arkansasstateparks.com/

TABLE OF CONTENTS

Arkansas County Park Map

Mark the places on the map where you have visited. Be creative use a sticker, or just put a dot to mark your journey.

Arkansas State Park Map

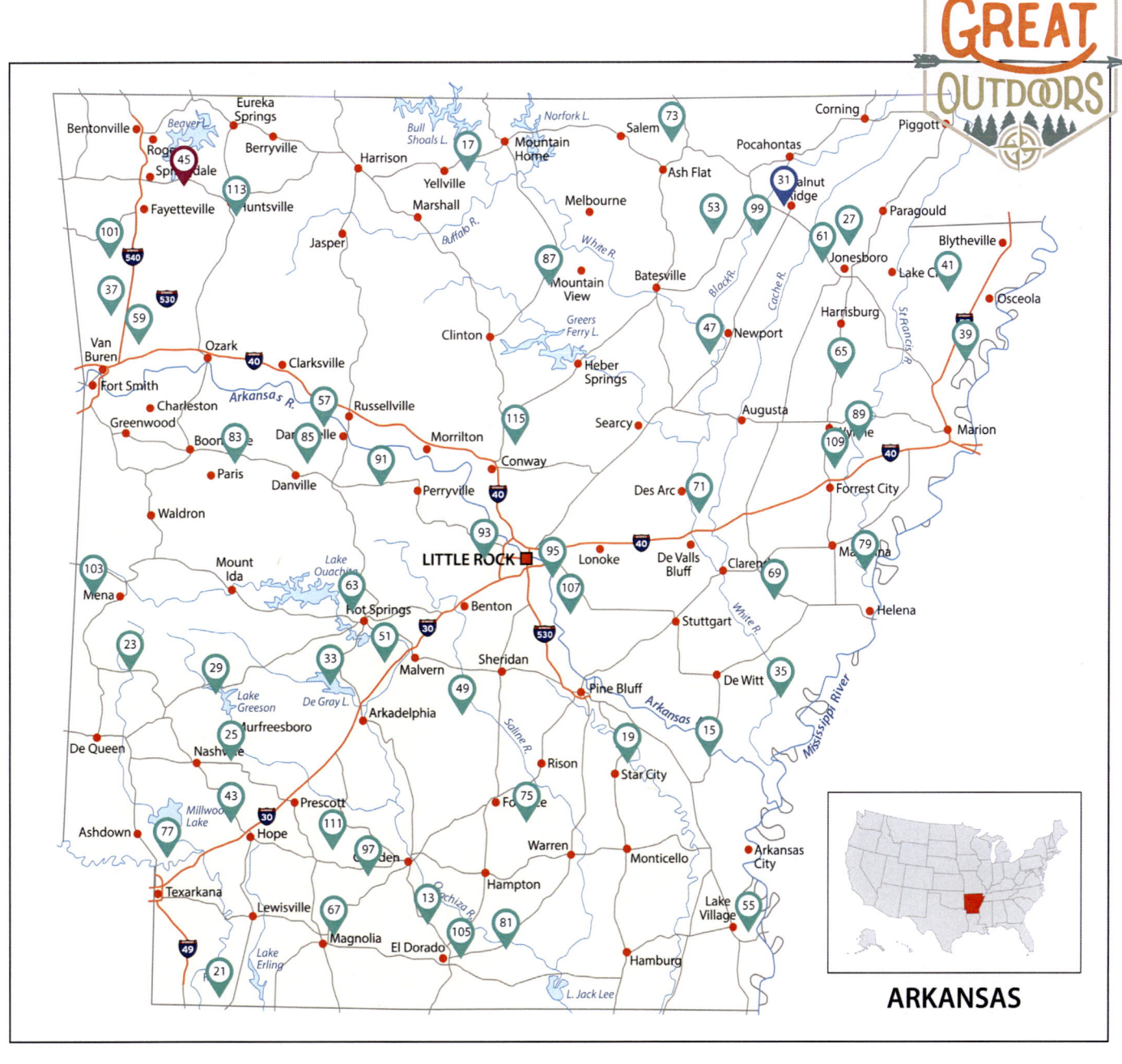

Mark the places on the map where you have visited. Be creative use a sticker, or just put a dot to mark your journey.

What you will find at the parks...

Petit Jean State Park

Website: https://www.arkansasstateparks.com/

ADVENTURE LIST

- [ ] Go on a nature scavenger hunt
- [ ] Perfect your bird calls
- [ ] Have a breakfast picnic
- [ ] Go horseback riding
- [ ] Snap a selfie at a park entrance sign
- [ ] Help Someone become a Jr Ranger
- [ ] Go RVing
- [ ] Take a ranger-led tour
- [ ] Splash in a waterfall
- [ ] Stop at scenic overlooks
- [ ] Hunt for fossils
- [ ] Look for EarthCache sites
- [ ] Canoe along a river
- [ ] Go on a photography walk
- [ ] Take a nature hike
- [ ] Hunt for animal tracks
- [ ] Go kayaking
- [ ] Try rock climbing
- [ ] Visit a nature center
- [ ] Watch the sunset
- [ ] Ride a bike
- [ ] Try a night sky program
- [ ] Go geocaching
- [ ] Pitch a tent
- [ ] Photograph wildflowers

- [ ] Cast a fishing line
- [ ] Take a boat cruise across a lake
- [ ] Enjoy a scenic drive
- [ ] Snap lots of photos
- [ ] Smell the fresh air
- [ ] Arrive early for wildlife watching
- [ ] Scramble over rocks
- [ ] Eat a picnic at a scenic spot
- [ ] Go on a night hike
- [ ] Ride a historic train
- [ ] Hike to the top of a mountain
- [ ] Try a cell phone audio tour
- [ ] Enjoy a tidepool walk
- [ ] Go on a full moon ranger hike
- [ ] Go on a cave tour
- [ ] Go stargazing
- [ ] Adhere to Leave No Trace principles
- [ ] Play in the water

EXPLORE MORE

☐ Trip Plan Completed

☐ Day Trip ☐ Overnight Stay

Reservations required: ☐ y ☐ n

Date reservations made: _____

Refund Policy: ☐ y ☐ n Site/Room #: _____

Confirmation #: _____

Miles to travel: _____

Time traveling: _____

Dog friendly?: ☐ y ☐ n

PLACES WE DISCOVERED ALONG THE WAY

PLACES TO STOP AND SEE ALONG THE WAY

Would you go again?: ☐ y ☐ n   Open all year?: ☐ y ☐ n

Activities Accomplished:

☐ Archery
☐ Biking
☐ Birding
☐ Boating
☐ Camping
☐ Caving
☐ Geocaching

☐ Fishing
☐ Hiking
☐ Horseback Riding
☐ Hunting
☐ Off-Roading
☐ Paddle Boarding
☐ Photography

☐ Picnicking
☐ Rock Climbing
☐ Shooting Range
☐ Snowshoeing
☐ Stargazing
☐ Swimming
☐ Tennis

☐ Walking
☐ Wildlife Watching
☐ _____
☐ _____
☐ _____
☐ _____
☐ _____

Traveled by:

☐ ☐ ☐ ☐ ☐ ☐ ☐ ☐ ☐ ☐ ☐ ☐

Add your favorite ticket stub, postcard, photo, stamp or drawing here

LET NEW ADVENTURES
>>> BEGIN →

ARKANSAS MUSEUM OF NATURAL RESOURCES

Address: 4087 Smackover Hwy. | Smackover, AR 71762

Website: https://www.arkansasstateparks.com/parks/arkansas-museum-natural-resources

Phone: 870-725-2877

Email: museumnaturalresources@arkansas.com

Established: 1986

Size: 19 acres (8 ha)

Star Rating
☆☆☆☆☆

What souvenir did you bring home?... _____

My favorite thing about this place is... _____

_____

Why I went ... _____

Who I went with ... _____

When I went ... _____

_____

What I did... _____

What I saw... _____

_____

What I learned... _____

_____

_____

An unforgettable moment... _____

_____

_____

A laughable moment... _____

_____

A surprising moment... _____

_____

_____

An unforeseeable moment... _____

_____

My List

- [ ] _____
- [ ] _____
- [ ] _____
- [ ] _____
- [ ] _____
- [ ] _____
- [ ] _____
- [ ] _____
- [ ] _____
- [ ] _____
- [ ] _____
- [ ] _____

Snapped a selfie | Location... _____

Took a park sign selfie? - Y | N

The weather was ...

☐ Trip Plan Completed

☐ Day Trip   ☐ Overnight Stay

Reservations required: ☐y ☐n

Date reservations made: _____

Refund Policy: ☐y ☐n Site/Room #: ____

Confirmation #: _____

Miles to travel: _____

Time traveling: _____

Dog friendly?: ☐y ☐n

PLACES WE DISCOVERED ALONG THE WAY

PLACES TO STOP AND SEE ALONG THE WAY

Would you go again?: ☐y ☐n   Open all year?: ☐y ☐n

Activities Accomplished:

☐ Archery
☐ Biking
☐ Birding
☐ Boating
☐ Camping
☐ Caving
☐ Geocaching

☐ Fishing
☐ Hiking
☐ Horseback Riding
☐ Hunting
☐ Off-Roading
☐ Paddle Boarding
☐ Photography

☐ Picnicking
☐ Rock Climbing
☐ Shooting Range
☐ Snowshoeing
☐ Stargazing
☐ Swimming
☐ Tennis

☐ Walking
☐ Wildlife Watching
☐ _____
☐ _____
☐ _____
☐ _____
☐ _____

Traveled by:

☐ ☐ ☐ ☐ ☐ ☐ ☐ ☐ ☐ ☐ ☐ ☐

Add your favorite ticket stub, postcard, photo, stamp or drawing here

NOT ALL THOSE WHO WANDER ARE LOST

ARKANSAS POST MUSEUM

Address: 5530 Hwy. 165 South | Gillett, AR 72055

Website: https://www.arkansasstateparks.com/parks/arkansas-post-museum

Phone: 870-548-2634

Email: arkansaspostmuseum@arkansas.com

Established: 1997

Size: 8 acres (3.2 ha)

Star Rating
☆☆☆☆☆

What souvenir did you bring home?...

My favorite thing about this place is...

Why I went ...

Who I went with ...

When I went ...

What I did...

What I saw...

What I learned...

An unforgettable moment...

A laughable moment...

A surprising moment...

An unforeseeable moment...

My List

- ☐
- ☐
- ☐
- ☐
- ☐
- ☐
- ☐
- ☐
- ☐
- ☐
- ☐
- ☐

Snapped a selfie | Location...

Took a park sign selfie? - Y | N

The weather was ...

PLAN YOUR TRIP:

☐ Trip Plan Completed

☐ Day Trip ☐ Overnight Stay

Reservations required: ☐y ☐n

Date reservations made: _____

Refund Policy: ☐y ☐n Site/Room #: _____

Confirmation #: _____

Miles to travel: _____

Time traveling: _____

Dog friendly?: ☐y ☐n

Activities Accomplished:

☐ Archery
☐ Biking
☐ Birding
☐ Boating
☐ Camping
☐ Caving
☐ Geocaching

☐ Fishing
☐ Hiking
☐ Horseback Riding
☐ Hunting
☐ Off-Roading
☐ Paddle Boarding
☐ Photography

☐ Picnicking
☐ Rock Climbing
☐ Shooting Range
☐ Snowshoeing
☐ Stargazing
☐ Swimming
☐ Tennis

☐ Walking
☐ Wildlife Watching
☐ _____
☐ _____
☐ _____
☐ _____
☐ _____

DESTINATION INFORMATION:

_____

PLACES WE DISCOVERED ALONG THE WAY

_____

_____

PLACES TO STOP AND SEE ALONG THE WAY

_____

_____

Would you go again?: ☐y ☐n   Open all year?: ☐y ☐n

Traveled by:

☐ ☐ ☐ ☐ ☐ ☐ ☐ ☐ ☐ ☐ ☐ ☐

Add your favorite ticket stub, postcard, photo, stamp or drawing here

LET NEW ADVENTURES
»› BEGIN →

16

BULL SHOALS-WHITE RIVER STATE PARK

Address: 153 Dam Overlook Lane | Bull Shoals, AR 72619

Website: https://www.arkansasstateparks.com/parks/bull-shoals-white-river-state-park

Phone: 870-445-3629

Email: bullshoalswhiteriver@arkansas.com

Established: 1955

Size: 732 acres (296 ha)

Star Rating
☆☆☆☆☆

What souvenir did you bring home?... _____

My favorite thing about this place is... _____

Why I went ... _____

Who I went with ... _____

When I went ... _____

What I did... _____

What I saw... _____

What I learned... _____

An unforgettable moment... _____

A laughable moment... _____

A surprising moment... _____

An unforeseeable moment... _____

My List

☐ _____
☐ _____
☐ _____
☐ _____
☐ _____
☐ _____
☐ _____
☐ _____
☐ _____
☐ _____
☐ _____

Snapped a selfie | Location... _____

Took a park sign selfie? - Y | N

The weather was ...

- ☐ Trip Plan Completed
- ☐ Day Trip ☐ Overnight Stay

Reservations required: ☐y ☐n

Date reservations made: _____

Refund Policy: ☐y ☐n Site/Room #: _____

Confirmation #: _____

Miles to travel: _____

Time traveling: _____

Dog friendly?: ☐y ☐n

PLACES WE DISCOVERED ALONG THE WAY

PLACES TO STOP AND SEE ALONG THE WAY

Would you go again?: ☐y ☐n   Open all year?: ☐y ☐n

Activities Accomplished:

- ☐ Archery
- ☐ Biking
- ☐ Birding
- ☐ Boating
- ☐ Camping
- ☐ Caving
- ☐ Geocaching

- ☐ Fishing
- ☐ Hiking
- ☐ Horseback Riding
- ☐ Hunting
- ☐ Off-Roading
- ☐ Paddle Boarding
- ☐ Photography

- ☐ Picnicking
- ☐ Rock Climbing
- ☐ Shooting Range
- ☐ Snowshoeing
- ☐ Stargazing
- ☐ Swimming
- ☐ Tennis

- ☐ Walking
- ☐ Wildlife Watching
- ☐ _____
- ☐ _____
- ☐ _____
- ☐ _____
- ☐ _____

Traveled by:

☐ ☐ ☐ ☐ ☐ ☐ ☐ ☐ ☐ ☐ ☐ ☐

Add your favorite ticket stub, postcard, photo, stamp or drawing here

NOT ALL THOSE WHO WANDER ARE LOST

CANE CREEK STATE PARK

Address: 50 State Park Road | Star City, AR 71667

Website: https://www.arkansasstateparks.com/parks/cane-creek-state-park

Phone: 870-628-4714

Email: canecreek@arkansas.com

Established: 1992

Size: 2,053 acres (831 ha)

Star Rating
☆☆☆☆☆

What souvenir did you bring home?... _____

My favorite thing about this place is... _____

Why I went ... _____

Who I went with ... _____

When I went ... _____

What I did... _____

What I saw... _____

What I learned... _____

An unforgettable moment... _____

A laughable moment... _____

A surprising moment... _____

An unforeseeable moment... _____

My List
- ☐ _____
- ☐ _____
- ☐ _____
- ☐ _____
- ☐ _____
- ☐ _____
- ☐ _____
- ☐ _____
- ☐ _____
- ☐ _____
- ☐ _____

Snapped a selfie | Location... _____

Took a park sign selfie? - Y | N   The weather was ...

PLAN YOUR TRIP:

- ☐ Trip Plan Completed
- ☐ Day Trip   ☐ Overnight Stay

Reservations required: ☐ y ☐ n

Date reservations made: _____

Refund Policy: ☐ y ☐ n   Site/Room #: _____

Confirmation #: _____

Miles to travel: _____

Time traveling: _____

Dog friendly?: ☐ y ☐ n

Activities Accomplished:

☐ Archery	☐ Fishing	☐ Picnicking	☐ Walking
☐ Biking	☐ Hiking	☐ Rock Climbing	☐ Wildlife Watching
☐ Birding	☐ Horseback Riding	☐ Shooting Range	☐ _____
☐ Boating	☐ Hunting	☐ Snowshoeing	☐ _____
☐ Camping	☐ Off-Roading	☐ Stargazing	☐ _____
☐ Caving	☐ Paddle Boarding	☐ Swimming	☐ _____
☐ Geocaching	☐ Photography	☐ Tennis	☐ _____

Traveled by:

☐ ☐ ☐ ☐ ☐ ☐ ☐ ☐ ☐ ☐ ☐ ☐

DESTINATION INFORMATION:

_____

PLACES WE DISCOVERED ALONG THE WAY

_____

_____

_____

PLACES TO STOP AND SEE ALONG THE WAY

_____

_____

_____

Would you go again?: ☐ y ☐ n   Open all year?: ☐ y ☐ n

Add your favorite ticket stub, postcard, photo, stamp or drawing here

LET NEW ADVENTURES
»» BEGIN →

CONWAY CEMETERY STATE PARK

Address: 33¬∞06'07.1"N 93¬∞41'00.9"W | Bradley, AR 71826

Website: https://www.arkansasstateparks.com/parks/conway-cemetery-state-park

Phone: (870) 695-3561

Email: conwaycemetery@arkansas.com

Established: 1986

Size: 11.5 acres (5 ha)

Star Rating
☆☆☆☆☆

What souvenir did you bring home?...

My favorite thing about this place is...

Why I went ...

Who I went with ...

When I went ...

What I did...

What I saw...

What I learned...

An unforgettable moment...

A laughable moment...

A surprising moment...

An unforeseeable moment...

My List

- [ ]
- [ ]
- [ ]
- [ ]
- [ ]
- [ ]
- [ ]
- [ ]
- [ ]
- [ ]
- [ ]
- [ ]

Snapped a selfie | Location...

Took a park sign selfie? - Y | N

The weather was ...

PLAN YOUR TRIP:

DESTINATION INFORMATION:

☐ Trip Plan Completed

☐ Day Trip   ☐ Overnight Stay

Reservations required: ☐y ☐n

Date reservations made: _____

Refund Policy: ☐y ☐n Site/Room #: _____

Confirmation #: _____

Miles to travel: _____

Time traveling: _____

Dog friendly?: ☐y ☐n

PLACES WE DISCOVERED ALONG THE WAY

PLACES TO STOP AND SEE ALONG THE WAY

Would you go again?: ☐y ☐n   Open all year?: ☐y ☐n

Activities Accomplished:

☐ Archery
☐ Biking
☐ Birding
☐ Boating
☐ Camping
☐ Caving
☐ Geocaching

☐ Fishing
☐ Hiking
☐ Horseback Riding
☐ Hunting
☐ Off-Roading
☐ Paddle Boarding
☐ Photography

☐ Picnicking
☐ Rock Climbing
☐ Shooting Range
☐ Snowshoeing
☐ Stargazing
☐ Swimming
☐ Tennis

☐ Walking
☐ Wildlife Watching
☐ _____
☐ _____
☐ _____
☐ _____
☐ _____

Traveled by:

☐ ☐ ☐ ☐ ☐ ☐ ☐ ☐ ☐ ☐ ☐ ☐

Add your favorite ticket stub, postcard, photo, stamp or drawing here

Cossatot River State Park-Natural Area

Address: 1980 Hwy. 278 West | Wickes, AR 71973

Website: https://www.arkansasstateparks.com/parks/cossatot-river-state-park-natural-area

Phone: 870-385-2201

Established: 1988

Email: cossatotriver@arkansas.com

Size: 5,230 acres (2145 ha)

What souvenir did you bring home?... _____

Star Rating
☆☆☆☆☆

My favorite thing about this place is... _____

Why I went ... _____

Who I went with ... _____

When I went ... _____

What I did... _____

What I saw... _____

What I learned... _____

An unforgettable moment... _____

A laughable moment... _____

A surprising moment... _____

An unforeseeable moment... _____

My List
- [ ] _____
- [ ] _____
- [ ] _____
- [ ] _____
- [ ] _____
- [ ] _____
- [ ] _____
- [ ] _____
- [ ] _____
- [ ] _____
- [ ] _____

 Snapped a selfie | Location... _____

 Took a park sign selfie? - Y | N

The weather was ...

- ☐ Trip Plan Completed
- ☐ Day Trip   ☐ Overnight Stay

Reservations required: ☐y ☐n

Date reservations made: _____

Refund Policy: ☐y ☐n Site/Room #: _____

Confirmation #: _____

Miles to travel: _____

Time traveling: _____

Dog friendly?: ☐y ☐n

_____

PLACES WE DISCOVERED ALONG THE WAY

_____
_____
_____

PLACES TO STOP AND SEE ALONG THE WAY

_____
_____

Would you go again? ☐y ☐n   Open all year? ☐y ☐n

Activities Accomplished:

- ☐ Archery
- ☐ Biking
- ☐ Birding
- ☐ Boating
- ☐ Camping
- ☐ Caving
- ☐ Geocaching

- ☐ Fishing
- ☐ Hiking
- ☐ Horseback Riding
- ☐ Hunting
- ☐ Off-Roading
- ☐ Paddle Boarding
- ☐ Photography

- ☐ Picnicking
- ☐ Rock Climbing
- ☐ Shooting Range
- ☐ Snowshoeing
- ☐ Stargazing
- ☐ Swimming
- ☐ Tennis

- ☐ Walking
- ☐ Wildlife Watching
- ☐ _____
- ☐ _____
- ☐ _____
- ☐ _____
- ☐ _____

Traveled by:

☐ ☐ ☐ ☐ ☐ ☐ ☐ ☐ ☐ ☐ ☐ ☐

Add your favorite ticket stub, postcard, photo, stamp or drawing here

LET NEW ADVENTURES
»> BEGIN →

CRATER OF DIAMONDS STATE PARK

Address: 209 State Park Rd | Murfreesboro, AR 71958

Website: https://www.arkansasstateparks.com/parks/crater-diamonds-state-park

Phone: 870-285-3113

Email: CraterofDiamonds@arkansas.com

Established: 1972

Size: 911 acres (369 ha)

Star Rating
☆☆☆☆☆

What souvenir did you bring home?... _____

My favorite thing about this place is... _____

Why I went ... _____

Who I went with ... _____

When I went ... _____

What I did... _____

What I saw... _____

What I learned... _____

An unforgettable moment... _____

A laughable moment... _____

A surprising moment... _____

An unforeseeable moment... _____

My List

- ☐ _____
- ☐ _____
- ☐ _____
- ☐ _____
- ☐ _____
- ☐ _____
- ☐ _____
- ☐ _____
- ☐ _____
- ☐ _____
- ☐ _____

Snapped a selfie | Location... _____

Took a park sign selfie? - Y | N   The weather was ...

PLAN YOUR TRIP:

DESTINATION INFORMATION:

☐ Trip Plan Completed

☐ Day Trip   ☐ Overnight Stay

Reservations required: ☐ y ☐ n

Date reservations made: _____

Refund Policy: ☐ y ☐ n Site/Room #: _____

Confirmation #: _____

Miles to travel: _____

Time traveling: _____

Dog friendly?: ☐ y ☐ n

PLACES WE DISCOVERED ALONG THE WAY

PLACES TO STOP AND SEE ALONG THE WAY

Would you go again?: ☐ y ☐ n   Open all year?: ☐ y ☐ n

Activities Accomplished:

☐ Archery
☐ Biking
☐ Birding
☐ Boating
☐ Camping
☐ Caving
☐ Geocaching

☐ Fishing
☐ Hiking
☐ Horseback Riding
☐ Hunting
☐ Off-Roading
☐ Paddle Boarding
☐ Photography

☐ Picnicking
☐ Rock Climbing
☐ Shooting Range
☐ Snowshoeing
☐ Stargazing
☐ Swimming
☐ Tennis

☐ Walking
☐ Wildlife Watching
☐ _____
☐ _____
☐ _____
☐ _____
☐ _____

Traveled by:

☐ ☐ ☐ ☐ ☐ ☐ ☐ ☐ ☐ ☐ ☐ ☐

Add your favorite ticket stub, postcard, photo, stamp or drawing here

NOT ALL THOSE WHO WANDER ARE LOST

Crowley's Ridge State Park

Address: 2092 Hwy. 168 North | Paragould, AR 72450

Website: https://www.arkansasstateparks.com/parks/crowleys-ridge-state-park

Phone: 870-573-6751

Email: crowleysridge@arkansas.com

Established: 1937

Size: 291 acres (118 ha)

Star Rating
☆ ☆ ☆ ☆ ☆

What souvenir did you bring home?...

My favorite thing about this place is...

Why I went ...

Who I went with ...

When I went ...

What I did...

What I saw...

What I learned...

An unforgettable moment...

A laughable moment...

A surprising moment...

An unforeseeable moment...

Snapped a selfie | Location...

Took a park sign selfie? - Y | N

My List

- ☐
- ☐
- ☐
- ☐
- ☐
- ☐
- ☐
- ☐
- ☐
- ☐
- ☐

The weather was ...

PLAN YOUR TRIP:

- ☐ Trip Plan Completed
- ☐ Day Trip ☐ Overnight Stay

Reservations required: ☐y ☐n

Date reservations made: _____

Refund Policy: ☐y ☐n Site/Room #: _____

Confirmation #: _____

Miles to travel: _____

Time traveling: _____

Dog friendly?: ☐y ☐n

Activities Accomplished:

- ☐ Archery
- ☐ Biking
- ☐ Birding
- ☐ Boating
- ☐ Camping
- ☐ Caving
- ☐ Geocaching

- ☐ Fishing
- ☐ Hiking
- ☐ Horseback Riding
- ☐ Hunting
- ☐ Off-Roading
- ☐ Paddle Boarding
- ☐ Photography

- ☐ Picnicking
- ☐ Rock Climbing
- ☐ Shooting Range
- ☐ Snowshoeing
- ☐ Stargazing
- ☐ Swimming
- ☐ Tennis

- ☐ Walking
- ☐ Wildlife Watching
- ☐ _____
- ☐ _____
- ☐ _____
- ☐ _____
- ☐ _____

Traveled by:

☐ ☐ ☐ ☐ ☐ ☐ ☐ ☐ ☐ ☐ ☐ ☐

DESTINATION INFORMATION:

_____

_____

PLACES WE DISCOVERED ALONG THE WAY

_____

_____

_____

PLACES TO STOP AND SEE ALONG THE WAY

_____

_____

_____

Would you go again?: ☐y ☐n   Open all year?: ☐y ☐n

Add your favorite ticket stub, postcard, photo, stamp or drawing here

LET NEW ADVENTURES
≫ BEGIN →

Daisy State Park

Address: 103 East Park | Kirby, AR 71950

Website: https://www.arkansasstateparks.com/parks/daisy-state-park

Phone: 870-398-4487

Email: daisy@arkansas.com

Established: 1955

Size: 276 acres (112 ha)

Star Rating
☆☆☆☆☆

What souvenir did you bring home?...

My favorite thing about this place is...

Why I went ...

Who I went with ...

When I went ...

What I did...

What I saw...

What I learned...

An unforgettable moment...

A laughable moment...

A surprising moment...

An unforeseeable moment...

Snapped a selfie | Location...

Took a park sign selfie? - Y | N

The weather was ...

My List
- [ ]
- [ ]
- [ ]
- [ ]
- [ ]
- [ ]
- [ ]
- [ ]
- [ ]
- [ ]
- [ ]

PLAN YOUR TRIP:

DESTINATION INFORMATION:

☐ Trip Plan Completed

☐ Day Trip ☐ Overnight Stay

Reservations required: ☐ y ☐ n

Date reservations made: _____

Refund Policy: ☐ y ☐ n Site/Room #: _____

Confirmation #: _____

Miles to travel: _____

Time traveling: _____

Dog friendly?: ☐ y ☐ n

PLACES WE DISCOVERED ALONG THE WAY

PLACES TO STOP AND SEE ALONG THE WAY

Would you go again?: ☐ y ☐ n   Open all year?: ☐ y ☐ n

Activities Accomplished:

☐ Archery
☐ Biking
☐ Birding
☐ Boating
☐ Camping
☐ Caving
☐ Geocaching

☐ Fishing
☐ Hiking
☐ Horseback Riding
☐ Hunting
☐ Off-Roading
☐ Paddle Boarding
☐ Photography

☐ Picnicking
☐ Rock Climbing
☐ Shooting Range
☐ Snowshoeing
☐ Stargazing
☐ Swimming
☐ Tennis

☐ Walking
☐ Wildlife Watching
☐ _____
☐ _____
☐ _____
☐ _____
☐ _____

Traveled by:

☐ ☐ ☐ ☐ ☐ ☐ ☐ ☐ ☐ ☐ ☐ ☐

Add your favorite ticket stub, postcard, photo, stamp or drawing here

NOT ALL THOSE WHO WANDER ARE LOST

Davidsonville Historic State Park

Address: 8047 Hwy. 166 South | Pocahontas, AR 72455

Website: https://www.arkansasstateparks.com/parks/davidsonville-historic-state-park

Phone: 870-892-4708

Email: davidsonville@arkansas.com

Established: 1957

Size: 163 acres (66 ha)

Star Rating
☆☆☆☆☆

What souvenir did you bring home?...

My favorite thing about this place is...

Why I went ...

Who I went with ...

When I went ...

What I did...

What I saw...

What I learned...

An unforgettable moment...

A laughable moment...

A surprising moment...

An unforeseeable moment...

My List

- ☐
- ☐
- ☐
- ☐
- ☐
- ☐
- ☐
- ☐
- ☐
- ☐
- ☐
- ☐

 Snapped a selfie | Location...

 Took a park sign selfie? - Y | N   The weather was ...

☐ Trip Plan Completed

☐ Day Trip   ☐ Overnight Stay

Reservations required: ☐y ☐n

Date reservations made: _____

Refund Policy: ☐y ☐n Site/Room #: _____

Confirmation #: _____

Miles to travel: _____

Time traveling: _____

Dog friendly?: ☐y ☐n

PLACES WE DISCOVERED ALONG THE WAY

PLACES TO STOP AND SEE ALONG THE WAY

Would you go again?: ☐y ☐n   Open all year?: ☐y ☐n

Activities Accomplished:

☐ Archery
☐ Biking
☐ Birding
☐ Boating
☐ Camping
☐ Caving
☐ Geocaching

☐ Fishing
☐ Hiking
☐ Horseback Riding
☐ Hunting
☐ Off-Roading
☐ Paddle Boarding
☐ Photography

☐ Picnicking
☐ Rock Climbing
☐ Shooting Range
☐ Snowshoeing
☐ Stargazing
☐ Swimming
☐ Tennis

☐ Walking
☐ Wildlife Watching
☐ _____
☐ _____
☐ _____
☐ _____
☐ _____

Traveled by:

☐ ☐ ☐ ☐ ☐ ☐ ☐ ☐ ☐ ☐ ☐ ☐

Add your favorite ticket stub, postcard, photo, stamp or drawing here

LET NEW ADVENTURES
»» BEGIN →

DeGray Lake Resort State Park

Address: 2027 State Park Entrance Road | Bismarck, AR 71929

Website: https://www.arkansasstateparks.com/parks/degray-lake-resort-state-park

Phone: 501-865-5850

Email: LRDeGray@arkansas.gov

Established: 1974

Size: 984 acres (398 ha)

Star Rating
☆☆☆☆☆

What souvenir did you bring home?...

My favorite thing about this place is...

Why I went ...

Who I went with ...

When I went ...

What I did...

What I saw...

What I learned...

An unforgettable moment...

A laughable moment...

A surprising moment...

An unforeseeable moment...

Snapped a selfie | Location...

Took a park sign selfie? - Y | N

The weather was ...

My List
- [ ]
- [ ]
- [ ]
- [ ]
- [ ]
- [ ]
- [ ]
- [ ]
- [ ]
- [ ]
- [ ]

PLAN YOUR TRIP:

DESTINATION INFORMATION:

☐ Trip Plan Completed

☐ Day Trip ☐ Overnight Stay

Reservations required: ☐y ☐n

Date reservations made: _____

Refund Policy: ☐y ☐n Site/Room #: _____

Confirmation #: _____

Miles to travel: _____

Time traveling: _____

Dog friendly?: ☐y ☐n

PLACES WE DISCOVERED ALONG THE WAY

PLACES TO STOP AND SEE ALONG THE WAY

Would you go again?: ☐y ☐n   Open all year?: ☐y ☐n

Activities Accomplished:

☐ Archery
☐ Biking
☐ Birding
☐ Boating
☐ Camping
☐ Caving
☐ Geocaching

☐ Fishing
☐ Hiking
☐ Horseback Riding
☐ Hunting
☐ Off-Roading
☐ Paddle Boarding
☐ Photography

☐ Picnicking
☐ Rock Climbing
☐ Shooting Range
☐ Snowshoeing
☐ Stargazing
☐ Swimming
☐ Tennis

☐ Walking
☐ Wildlife Watching
☐ _____
☐ _____
☐ _____
☐ _____
☐ _____

Traveled by:

☐ ☐ ☐ ☐ ☐ ☐ ☐ ☐ ☐ ☐ ☐ ☐

Add your favorite ticket stub, postcard, photo, stamp or drawing here

Delta Heritage Trail State Park

Address: 5539 Hwy 49 | Helena-West Helena, AR 72390

Website: https://www.arkansasstateparks.com/parks/delta-heritage-trail-state-park

Phone: 870-572-2352

Email: deltaheritagetrail@arkansas.com

Established: 2002

Size: 960 acres (390 ha)

Star Rating ☆☆☆☆☆

What souvenir did you bring home?...

My favorite thing about this place is...

Why I went ...

Who I went with ...

When I went ...

What I did...

What I saw...

What I learned...

An unforgettable moment...

A laughable moment...

A surprising moment...

An unforeseeable moment...

My List

- ☐
- ☐
- ☐
- ☐
- ☐
- ☐
- ☐
- ☐
- ☐
- ☐
- ☐
- ☐

Snapped a selfie | Location...

Took a park sign selfie? - Y | N

The weather was ...

☐ Trip Plan Completed

☐ Day Trip ☐ Overnight Stay

Reservations required: ☐y ☐n

Date reservations made: _____

Refund Policy: ☐y ☐n Site/Room #: _____

Confirmation #: _____

Miles to travel: _____

Time traveling: _____

Dog friendly?: ☐y ☐n

PLACES WE DISCOVERED ALONG THE WAY

PLACES TO STOP AND SEE ALONG THE WAY

Would you go again? ☐y ☐n   Open all year? ☐y ☐n

Activities Accomplished:

☐ Archery
☐ Biking
☐ Birding
☐ Boating
☐ Camping
☐ Caving
☐ Geocaching

☐ Fishing
☐ Hiking
☐ Horseback Riding
☐ Hunting
☐ Off-Roading
☐ Paddle Boarding
☐ Photography

☐ Picnicking
☐ Rock Climbing
☐ Shooting Range
☐ Snowshoeing
☐ Stargazing
☐ Swimming
☐ Tennis

☐ Walking
☐ Wildlife Watching
☐ _____
☐ _____
☐ _____
☐ _____
☐ _____

Traveled by:

☐ ☐ ☐ ☐ ☐ ☐ ☐ ☐ ☐ ☐ ☐ ☐

Add your favorite ticket stub, postcard, photo, stamp or drawing here

LET NEW ADVENTURES
»» BEGIN →

Devil's Den State Park

Address: 11333 West Arkansas Hwy. 74 | West Fork, AR 72774

Website: https://www.arkansasstateparks.com/parks/devils-den-state-park

Phone: 479-761-3325

Email: devilsden@arkansas.com

Established: 1933

Size: 2,500 acres (1000 ha)

Star Rating

☆ ☆ ☆ ☆ ☆

What souvenir did you bring home?...

My favorite thing about this place is...

Why I went ...

Who I went with ...

When I went ...

What I did...

What I saw...

What I learned...

An unforgettable moment...

A laughable moment...

A surprising moment...

An unforeseeable moment...

My List

- [ ]
- [ ]
- [ ]
- [ ]
- [ ]
- [ ]
- [ ]
- [ ]
- [ ]
- [ ]
- [ ]
- [ ]

 Snapped a selfie | Location...

Took a park sign selfie? - Y | N

The weather was ...

PLAN YOUR TRIP:

☐ Trip Plan Completed
☐ Day Trip   ☐ Overnight Stay
Reservations required: ☐ y ☐ n
Date reservations made: _____
Refund Policy: ☐ y ☐ n Site/Room #: _____
Confirmation #: _____
Miles to travel: _____
Time traveling: _____
Dog friendly?: ☐ y ☐ n

Activities Accomplished:

☐ Archery
☐ Biking
☐ Birding
☐ Boating
☐ Camping
☐ Caving
☐ Geocaching

☐ Fishing
☐ Hiking
☐ Horseback Riding
☐ Hunting
☐ Off-Roading
☐ Paddle Boarding
☐ Photography

☐ Picnicking
☐ Rock Climbing
☐ Shooting Range
☐ Snowshoeing
☐ Stargazing
☐ Swimming
☐ Tennis

☐ Walking
☐ Wildlife Watching
☐ _____
☐ _____
☐ _____
☐ _____
☐ _____

DESTINATION INFORMATION:

PLACES WE DISCOVERED ALONG THE WAY

PLACES TO STOP AND SEE ALONG THE WAY

Would you go again?: ☐ y ☐ n   Open all year?: ☐ y ☐ n

Traveled by:

☐ ☐ ☐ ☐ ☐ ☐ ☐ ☐ ☐ ☐ ☐ ☐

Add your favorite ticket stub, postcard, photo, stamp or drawing here

NOT ALL THOSE WHO WANDER ARE LOST

Hampson Archeological Museum State Park

Address: 33 Park Avenue | Wilson, AR 72395

Website: https://www.arkansasstateparks.com/parks/hampson-archeological-museum-state-park

Phone: 870-655-8622

Email: hampsonarcheologicalmuseum@arkansas.com

Established: 1961

Size: 5 acres (2 ha)

Star Rating
☆☆☆☆☆

What souvenir did you bring home?...

My favorite thing about this place is...

Why I went ...

Who I went with ...

When I went ...

What I did...

What I saw...

What I learned...

An unforgettable moment...

A laughable moment...

A surprising moment...

An unforeseeable moment...

Snapped a selfie | Location...

Took a park sign selfie? - Y | N

My List

- ☐
- ☐
- ☐
- ☐
- ☐
- ☐
- ☐
- ☐
- ☐
- ☐
- ☐
- ☐

The weather was ...

☐ Trip Plan Completed

☐ Day Trip ☐ Overnight Stay

Reservations required: ☐y ☐n

Date reservations made: _____

Refund Policy: ☐y ☐n Site/Room #: _____

Confirmation #: _____

Miles to travel: _____

Time traveling: _____

Dog friendly?: ☐y ☐n

PLACES WE DISCOVERED ALONG THE WAY

PLACES TO STOP AND SEE ALONG THE WAY

Would you go again?: ☐y ☐n   Open all year?: ☐y ☐n

Activities Accomplished:

☐ Archery
☐ Biking
☐ Birding
☐ Boating
☐ Camping
☐ Caving
☐ Geocaching

☐ Fishing
☐ Hiking
☐ Horseback Riding
☐ Hunting
☐ Off-Roading
☐ Paddle Boarding
☐ Photography

☐ Picnicking
☐ Rock Climbing
☐ Shooting Range
☐ Snowshoeing
☐ Stargazing
☐ Swimming
☐ Tennis

☐ Walking
☐ Wildlife Watching
☐ _____
☐ _____
☐ _____
☐ _____
☐ _____

Traveled by:

☐ ☐ ☐ ☐ ☐ ☐ ☐ ☐ ☐ ☐ ☐ ☐

Add your favorite ticket stub, postcard, photo, stamp or drawing here

LET NEW ADVENTURES
≫ BEGIN →

Herman Davis State Park

Address: "Corner of Ark. 18 and Baltimore Street | Manila, AR 72442"

Website: https://www.arkansasstateparks.com/parks/herman-davis-state-park

Phone: 888-287-2757

Email: hermandavis@arkansas.com

Established: 1953

Size: 1 acre (0.4 ha)

Star Rating
☆☆☆☆☆

What souvenir did you bring home?... _____

My favorite thing about this place is... _____

_____

Why I went ... _____

Who I went with ... _____

When I went ... _____

What I did... _____

What I saw... _____

_____

What I learned... _____

_____

An unforgettable moment... _____

_____

A laughable moment... _____

_____

A surprising moment... _____

_____

An unforeseeable moment... _____

_____

My List
- ☐ _____
- ☐ _____
- ☐ _____
- ☐ _____
- ☐ _____
- ☐ _____
- ☐ _____
- ☐ _____
- ☐ _____
- ☐ _____
- ☐ _____

Snapped a selfie | Location... _____

Took a park sign selfie? - Y | N   The weather was ...

- ☐ Trip Plan Completed
- ☐ Day Trip ☐ Overnight Stay

Reservations required: ☐ y ☐ n

Date reservations made: _____

Refund Policy: ☐ y ☐ n Site/Room #: _____

Confirmation #: _____

Miles to travel: _____

Time traveling: _____

Dog friendly?: ☐ y ☐ n

PLACES WE DISCOVERED ALONG THE WAY

PLACES TO STOP AND SEE ALONG THE WAY

Would you go again?: ☐ y ☐ n   Open all year?: ☐ y ☐ n

Activities Accomplished:

- ☐ Archery
- ☐ Biking
- ☐ Birding
- ☐ Boating
- ☐ Camping
- ☐ Caving
- ☐ Geocaching
- ☐ Fishing
- ☐ Hiking
- ☐ Horseback Riding
- ☐ Hunting
- ☐ Off-Roading
- ☐ Paddle Boarding
- ☐ Photography
- ☐ Picnicking
- ☐ Rock Climbing
- ☐ Shooting Range
- ☐ Snowshoeing
- ☐ Stargazing
- ☐ Swimming
- ☐ Tennis
- ☐ Walking
- ☐ Wildlife Watching
- ☐ _____
- ☐ _____
- ☐ _____
- ☐ _____
- ☐ _____

Traveled by:

☐ ☐ ☐ ☐ ☐ ☐ ☐ ☐ ☐ ☐ ☐ ☐

Add your favorite ticket stub, postcard, photo, stamp or drawing here

NOT ALL THOSE WHO WANDER ARE LOST

Historic Washington State Park

Address: 103 Franklin Street | Washington, AR 71862

Website: https://www.arkansasstateparks.com/parks/historic-washington-state-park

Phone: 870-983-2684

Email: historicwashington@arkansas.com

Established: 1973

Size: 101 acres (41 ha)

Star Rating
☆☆☆☆☆

What souvenir did you bring home?... _____

My favorite thing about this place is... _____

_____

Why I went ... _____

Who I went with ... _____

When I went ... _____

What I did... _____

What I saw... _____

What I learned... _____

An unforgettable moment... _____

A laughable moment... _____

A surprising moment... _____

An unforeseeable moment... _____

My List

- [ ] _____
- [ ] _____
- [ ] _____
- [ ] _____
- [ ] _____
- [ ] _____
- [ ] _____
- [ ] _____
- [ ] _____
- [ ] _____
- [ ] _____
- [ ] _____

Snapped a selfie | Location... _____

Took a park sign selfie? - Y | N

The weather was ...

PLAN YOUR TRIP:

DESTINATION INFORMATION:

- ☐ Trip Plan Completed
- ☐ Day Trip   ☐ Overnight Stay

Reservations required: ☐y ☐n

Date reservations made: _____

Refund Policy: ☐y ☐n Site/Room #: _____

Confirmation #: _____

Miles to travel: _____

Time traveling: _____

Dog friendly?: ☐y ☐n

PLACES WE DISCOVERED ALONG THE WAY

_____

_____

PLACES TO STOP AND SEE ALONG THE WAY

_____

_____

Would you go again?: ☐y ☐n   Open all year?: ☐y ☐n

Activities Accomplished:

- ☐ Archery
- ☐ Biking
- ☐ Birding
- ☐ Boating
- ☐ Camping
- ☐ Caving
- ☐ Geocaching

- ☐ Fishing
- ☐ Hiking
- ☐ Horseback Riding
- ☐ Hunting
- ☐ Off-Roading
- ☐ Paddle Boarding
- ☐ Photography

- ☐ Picnicking
- ☐ Rock Climbing
- ☐ Shooting Range
- ☐ Snowshoeing
- ☐ Stargazing
- ☐ Swimming
- ☐ Tennis

- ☐ Walking
- ☐ Wildlife Watching
- ☐ _____
- ☐ _____
- ☐ _____
- ☐ _____
- ☐ _____

Traveled by:

☐ ☐ ☐ ☐ ☐ ☐ ☐ ☐ ☐ ☐ ☐ ☐

Add your favorite ticket stub, postcard, photo, stamp or drawing here

LET NEW ADVENTURES
»› BEGIN →

Hobbs State Park ‚Äì Conservation Area

Address: 20201 East Hwy. 12 | Rogers, AR 72756

Website: https://www.arkansasstateparks.com/parks/hobbs-state-park-conservation-area

Phone: 479-789-5000

Email: hobbs@arkansas.com

Established: 1979

Size: 12,056 acres (4879 ha)

Star Rating
☆☆☆☆☆

What souvenir did you bring home?...

My favorite thing about this place is...

Why I went ...

Who I went with ...

When I went ...

What I did...

What I saw...

What I learned...

An unforgettable moment...

A laughable moment...

A surprising moment...

An unforeseeable moment...

Snapped a selfie | Location...

Took a park sign selfie? - Y | N

The weather was ...

My List

- ☐
- ☐
- ☐
- ☐
- ☐
- ☐
- ☐
- ☐
- ☐
- ☐
- ☐
- ☐

PLAN YOUR TRIP:

DESTINATION INFORMATION:

☐ Trip Plan Completed
☐ Day Trip   ☐ Overnight Stay
Reservations required: ☐y ☐n
Date reservations made: _____
Refund Policy: ☐y ☐n Site/Room #: _____
Confirmation #: _____
Miles to travel: _____
Time traveling: _____
Dog friendly?: ☐y ☐n

PLACES WE DISCOVERED ALONG THE WAY

PLACES TO STOP AND SEE ALONG THE WAY

Activities Accomplished:

Would you go again?: ☐y ☐n   Open all year?: ☐y ☐n

☐ Archery
☐ Biking
☐ Birding
☐ Boating
☐ Camping
☐ Caving
☐ Geocaching

☐ Fishing
☐ Hiking
☐ Horseback Riding
☐ Hunting
☐ Off-Roading
☐ Paddle Boarding
☐ Photography

☐ Picnicking
☐ Rock Climbing
☐ Shooting Range
☐ Snowshoeing
☐ Stargazing
☐ Swimming
☐ Tennis

☐ Walking
☐ Wildlife Watching
☐ _____
☐ _____
☐ _____
☐ _____
☐ _____

Traveled by:

☐ ☐ ☐ ☐ ☐ ☐ ☐ ☐ ☐ ☐ ☐ ☐

Add your favorite ticket stub, postcard, photo, stamp or drawing here

NOT ALL THOSE WHO WANDER ARE LOST

46

Jacksonport State Park

Address: 111 Avenue St. | Newport, AR 72112

Website: https://www.arkansasstateparks.com/parks/jacksonport-state-park

Phone: 870-523-2143

Email: jacksonport@arkansas.com

Established: 1965

Size: 164.7 acres (66.7 ha)

Star Rating ☆☆☆☆☆

What souvenir did you bring home?... _____

My favorite thing about this place is... _____

_____

Why I went ... _____

Who I went with ... _____

When I went ... _____

_____

What I did... _____

What I saw... _____

_____

What I learned... _____

_____

An unforgettable moment... _____

_____

A laughable moment... _____

_____

A surprising moment... _____

_____

An unforeseeable moment... _____

_____

My List

- ☐ _____
- ☐ _____
- ☐ _____
- ☐ _____
- ☐ _____
- ☐ _____
- ☐ _____
- ☐ _____
- ☐ _____
- ☐ _____
- ☐ _____
- ☐ _____

 Snapped a selfie | Location... _____

 Took a park sign selfie? - Y | N

 The weather was ...

☐ Trip Plan Completed
☐ Day Trip   ☐ Overnight Stay
Reservations required: ☐y ☐n
Date reservations made: _____
Refund Policy: ☐y ☐n Site/Room #: _____
Confirmation #: _____
Miles to travel: _____
Time traveling: _____
Dog friendly?: ☐y ☐n

_____

PLACES WE DISCOVERED ALONG THE WAY

_____
_____
_____

PLACES TO STOP AND SEE ALONG THE WAY

_____
_____
_____

Activities Accomplished:

Would you go again?: ☐y ☐n   Open all year?: ☐y ☐n

☐ Archery
☐ Biking
☐ Birding
☐ Boating
☐ Camping
☐ Caving
☐ Geocaching

☐ Fishing
☐ Hiking
☐ Horseback Riding
☐ Hunting
☐ Off-Roading
☐ Paddle Boarding
☐ Photography

☐ Picnicking
☐ Rock Climbing
☐ Shooting Range
☐ Snowshoeing
☐ Stargazing
☐ Swimming
☐ Tennis

☐ Walking
☐ Wildlife Watching
☐ _____
☐ _____
☐ _____
☐ _____
☐ _____

Traveled by:

☐ ☐ ☐ ☐ ☐ ☐ ☐ ☐ ☐ ☐ ☐ ☐

Add your favorite ticket stub, postcard, photo, stamp or drawing here

LET NEW ADVENTURES
»» BEGIN →

Jenkins' Ferry Battleground State Park

Address: Co Rd 317/Forest Rd 9010 | Leola, AR 72084

Website: https://www.arkansasstateparks.com/parks/jenkins-ferry-battleground-state-park

Phone: 888-287-2757

Email: jenkinsferry@arkansas.com

Established: 1961

Size: 40 acres (16.2 ha)

Star Rating
☆☆☆☆☆

What souvenir did you bring home?... _____

My favorite thing about this place is... _____

Why I went ... _____

Who I went with ... _____

When I went ... _____

What I did... _____

What I saw... _____

What I learned... _____

An unforgettable moment... _____

A laughable moment... _____

A surprising moment... _____

An unforeseeable moment... _____

My List

- [ ] _____
- [ ] _____
- [ ] _____
- [ ] _____
- [ ] _____
- [ ] _____
- [ ] _____
- [ ] _____
- [ ] _____
- [ ] _____
- [ ] _____

 Snapped a selfie | Location... _____

 Took a park sign selfie? - Y | N

The weather was ...

PLAN YOUR TRIP:

DESTINATION INFORMATION:

☐ Trip Plan Completed

☐ Day Trip ☐ Overnight Stay

Reservations required: ☐y ☐n

Date reservations made: _____

Refund Policy: ☐y ☐n Site/Room #: _____

Confirmation #: _____

Miles to travel: _____

Time traveling: _____

Dog friendly?: ☐y ☐n

_____

PLACES WE DISCOVERED ALONG THE WAY

_____
_____
_____

PLACES TO STOP AND SEE ALONG THE WAY

_____
_____
_____

Activities Accomplished:

Would you go again?: ☐y ☐n   Open all year?: ☐y ☐n

☐ Archery
☐ Biking
☐ Birding
☐ Boating
☐ Camping
☐ Caving
☐ Geocaching

☐ Fishing
☐ Hiking
☐ Horseback Riding
☐ Hunting
☐ Off-Roading
☐ Paddle Boarding
☐ Photography

☐ Picnicking
☐ Rock Climbing
☐ Shooting Range
☐ Snowshoeing
☐ Stargazing
☐ Swimming
☐ Tennis

☐ Walking
☐ Wildlife Watching
☐ _____
☐ _____
☐ _____
☐ _____
☐ _____

Traveled by:

☐ ☐ ☐ ☐ ☐ ☐ ☐ ☐ ☐ ☐ ☐ ☐

Add your favorite ticket stub, postcard, photo, stamp or drawing here

Lake Catherine State Park

Address: 1200 Catherine Park Road | Hot Springs, AR 71913

Website: https://www.arkansasstateparks.com/parks/lake-catherine-state-park

Phone: 501-844-4176

Email: lakecatherine@arkansas.com

Established: 1935

Size: 2,180 acres (882.2 ha)

Star Rating
☆ ☆ ☆ ☆ ☆

What souvenir did you bring home?... _____

My favorite thing about this place is... _____

Why I went ... _____

Who I went with ... _____

When I went ... _____

What I did... _____

What I saw... _____

What I learned... _____

An unforgettable moment... _____

A laughable moment... _____

A surprising moment... _____

An unforeseeable moment... _____

My List
- [ ] _____
- [ ] _____
- [ ] _____
- [ ] _____
- [ ] _____
- [ ] _____
- [ ] _____
- [ ] _____
- [ ] _____
- [ ] _____
- [ ] _____

Snapped a selfie | Location... _____

Took a park sign selfie? - Y | N

The weather was ...

☐ Trip Plan Completed

☐ Day Trip ☐ Overnight Stay

Reservations required: ☐y ☐n

Date reservations made: _____

Refund Policy: ☐y ☐n Site/Room #: _____

Confirmation #: _____

Miles to travel: _____

Time traveling: _____

Dog friendly?: ☐y ☐n

PLACES WE DISCOVERED ALONG THE WAY

PLACES TO STOP AND SEE ALONG THE WAY

Would you go again?: ☐y ☐n   Open all year?: ☐y ☐n

Activities Accomplished:

☐ Archery
☐ Biking
☐ Birding
☐ Boating
☐ Camping
☐ Caving
☐ Geocaching

☐ Fishing
☐ Hiking
☐ Horseback Riding
☐ Hunting
☐ Off-Roading
☐ Paddle Boarding
☐ Photography

☐ Picnicking
☐ Rock Climbing
☐ Shooting Range
☐ Snowshoeing
☐ Stargazing
☐ Swimming
☐ Tennis

☐ Walking
☐ Wildlife Watching
☐ _____
☐ _____
☐ _____
☐ _____
☐ _____

Traveled by:

☐ ☐ ☐ ☐ ☐ ☐ ☐ ☐ ☐ ☐ ☐ ☐

Add your favorite ticket stub, postcard, photo, stamp or drawing here

LET NEW ADVENTURES
≫ BEGIN →

Lake Charles State Park

Address: 3705 Hwy. 25 | Powhatan, AR 72458

Website: https://www.arkansasstateparks.com/parks/lake-charles-state-park

Phone: 870-878-6595

Email: lakecharles@arkansas.com

Established: 1967

Size: 140 acres (57 ha)

Star Rating
☆☆☆☆☆

What souvenir did you bring home?...

My favorite thing about this place is...

Why I went ...

Who I went with ...

When I went ...

What I did...

What I saw...

What I learned...

An unforgettable moment...

A laughable moment...

A surprising moment...

An unforeseeable moment...

My List
- ☐
- ☐
- ☐
- ☐
- ☐
- ☐
- ☐
- ☐
- ☐
- ☐
- ☐

Snapped a selfie | Location...

Took a park sign selfie? - Y | N

The weather was ...

☐ Trip Plan Completed

☐ Day Trip   ☐ Overnight Stay

Reservations required: ☐y ☐n

Date reservations made: _____

Refund Policy: ☐y ☐n Site/Room #: ___

Confirmation #: _____

Miles to travel: _____

Time traveling: _____

Dog friendly?: ☐y ☐n

PLACES WE DISCOVERED ALONG THE WAY

PLACES TO STOP AND SEE ALONG THE WAY

Would you go again?: ☐y ☐n   Open all year?: ☐y ☐n

Activities Accomplished:

☐ Archery
☐ Biking
☐ Birding
☐ Boating
☐ Camping
☐ Caving
☐ Geocaching

☐ Fishing
☐ Hiking
☐ Horseback Riding
☐ Hunting
☐ Off-Roading
☐ Paddle Boarding
☐ Photography

☐ Picnicking
☐ Rock Climbing
☐ Shooting Range
☐ Snowshoeing
☐ Stargazing
☐ Swimming
☐ Tennis

☐ Walking
☐ Wildlife Watching
☐ _____
☐ _____
☐ _____
☐ _____
☐ _____

Traveled by:

☐ ☐ ☐ ☐ ☐ ☐ ☐ ☐ ☐ ☐ ☐ ☐

Add your favorite ticket stub, postcard, photo, stamp or drawing here

NOT ALL THOSE WHO WANDER ARE LOST

N W E S

LAKE CHICOT STATE PARK

Address: 2542 Hwy. 257 | Lake Village, AR 71653

Website: https://www.arkansasstateparks.com/parks/lake-chicot-state-park

Phone: 870-265-5480

Email: lakechicot@arkansas.com

Established: 1957

Size: 211.6 acres (85.6 ha)

Star Rating
☆☆☆☆☆

What souvenir did you bring home?...

My favorite thing about this place is...

Why I went ...

Who I went with ...

When I went ...

What I did...

What I saw...

What I learned...

An unforgettable moment...

A laughable moment...

A surprising moment...

An unforeseeable moment...

My List

- ☐
- ☐
- ☐
- ☐
- ☐
- ☐
- ☐
- ☐
- ☐
- ☐
- ☐
- ☐

Snapped a selfie | Location...

Took a park sign selfie? - Y | N

The weather was ...

PLAN YOUR TRIP:

☐ Trip Plan Completed
☐ Day Trip   ☐ Overnight Stay
Reservations required: ☐y ☐n
Date reservations made: _____
Refund Policy: ☐y ☐n Site/Room #: _____
Confirmation #: _____
Miles to travel: _____
Time traveling: _____
Dog friendly?: ☐y ☐n

Activities Accomplished:

☐ Archery
☐ Biking
☐ Birding
☐ Boating
☐ Camping
☐ Caving
☐ Geocaching

☐ Fishing
☐ Hiking
☐ Horseback Riding
☐ Hunting
☐ Off-Roading
☐ Paddle Boarding
☐ Photography

☐ Picnicking
☐ Rock Climbing
☐ Shooting Range
☐ Snowshoeing
☐ Stargazing
☐ Swimming
☐ Tennis

☐ Walking
☐ Wildlife Watching
☐ _____
☐ _____
☐ _____
☐ _____
☐ _____

Traveled by:

☐ ☐ ☐ ☐ ☐ ☐ ☐ ☐ ☐ ☐ ☐ ☐

DESTINATION INFORMATION:

_____

PLACES WE DISCOVERED ALONG THE WAY

_____
_____
_____

PLACES TO STOP AND SEE ALONG THE WAY

_____
_____
_____

Would you go again?: ☐y ☐n   Open all year?: ☐y ☐n

Add your favorite ticket stub, postcard, photo, stamp or drawing here

LET NEW ADVENTURES
»» BEGIN →

Lake Dardanelle State Park

Address: 2428 Marina Rd | Russellville, AR 72802

Website: https://www.arkansasstateparks.com/parks/lake-dardanelle-state-park

Phone: 479-967-5516

Email: lakedardanelle@arkansas.com

Established: 1966

Size: 246 acres (99.6 ha)

What souvenir did you bring home?... _____

My favorite thing about this place is... _____

Star Rating
☆☆☆☆☆

Why I went ... _____

Who I went with ... _____

When I went ... _____

What I did... _____

What I saw... _____

What I learned... _____

An unforgettable moment... _____

A laughable moment... _____

A surprising moment... _____

An unforeseeable moment... _____

My List
- [ ] _____
- [ ] _____
- [ ] _____
- [ ] _____
- [ ] _____
- [ ] _____
- [ ] _____
- [ ] _____
- [ ] _____
- [ ] _____
- [ ] _____

Snapped a selfie | Location... _____

Took a park sign selfie? - Y | N

The weather was ...

PLAN YOUR TRIP:

DESTINATION INFORMATION:

☐ Trip Plan Completed

☐ Day Trip ☐ Overnight Stay

Reservations required: ☐y ☐n

Date reservations made: _____

Refund Policy: ☐y ☐n Site/Room #: _____

Confirmation #: _____

Miles to travel: _____

Time traveling: _____

Dog friendly?: ☐y ☐n

PLACES WE DISCOVERED ALONG THE WAY

PLACES TO STOP AND SEE ALONG THE WAY

Would you go again?: ☐y ☐n   Open all year?: ☐y ☐n

Activities Accomplished:

☐ Archery
☐ Biking
☐ Birding
☐ Boating
☐ Camping
☐ Caving
☐ Geocaching

☐ Fishing
☐ Hiking
☐ Horseback Riding
☐ Hunting
☐ Off-Roading
☐ Paddle Boarding
☐ Photography

☐ Picnicking
☐ Rock Climbing
☐ Shooting Range
☐ Snowshoeing
☐ Stargazing
☐ Swimming
☐ Tennis

☐ Walking
☐ Wildlife Watching
☐ _____
☐ _____
☐ _____
☐ _____
☐ _____

Traveled by:

☐ ☐ ☐ ☐ ☐ ☐ ☐ ☐ ☐ ☐ ☐ ☐

Add your favorite ticket stub, postcard, photo, stamp or drawing here

NOT ALL THOSE WHO WANDER ARE LOST

N W E S

Lake Fort Smith State Park

Address: 15458 Shepard Springs Road | Mountainburg, AR 72946-0004

Website: https://www.arkansasstateparks.com/parks/lake-fort-smith-state-park

Phone: 479-369-2469

Email: lakefortsmith@arkansas.com

Established: 1967

Size: 260 acres (105.2 ha)

What souvenir did you bring home?...

My favorite thing about this place is...

Star Rating
☆☆☆☆☆

Why I went ...

Who I went with ...

When I went ...

What I did...

What I saw...

What I learned...

An unforgettable moment...

A laughable moment...

A surprising moment...

My List

- [ ]
- [ ]
- [ ]
- [ ]
- [ ]
- [ ]
- [ ]
- [ ]
- [ ]
- [ ]
- [ ]

An unforeseeable moment...

Snapped a selfie | Location...

Took a park sign selfie? - Y | N

The weather was ...

PLAN YOUR TRIP:

DESTINATION INFORMATION:

☐ Trip Plan Completed

☐ Day Trip   ☐ Overnight Stay

Reservations required: ☐y ☐n

Date reservations made: _____

Refund Policy: ☐y ☐n   Site/Room #: _____

Confirmation #: _____

Miles to travel: _____

Time traveling: _____

Dog friendly?: ☐y ☐n

PLACES WE DISCOVERED ALONG THE WAY

PLACES TO STOP AND SEE ALONG THE WAY

Would you go again?: ☐y ☐n   Open all year?: ☐y ☐n

Activities Accomplished:

☐ Archery
☐ Biking
☐ Birding
☐ Boating
☐ Camping
☐ Caving
☐ Geocaching

☐ Fishing
☐ Hiking
☐ Horseback Riding
☐ Hunting
☐ Off-Roading
☐ Paddle Boarding
☐ Photography

☐ Picnicking
☐ Rock Climbing
☐ Shooting Range
☐ Snowshoeing
☐ Stargazing
☐ Swimming
☐ Tennis

☐ Walking
☐ Wildlife Watching
☐ _____
☐ _____
☐ _____
☐ _____
☐ _____

Traveled by:

☐ ☐ ☐ ☐ ☐ ☐ ☐ ☐ ☐ ☐ ☐ ☐

Add your favorite ticket stub, postcard, photo, stamp or drawing here

LET NEW ADVENTURES
≫ BEGIN →

Lake Frierson State Park

Address: 7904 Hwy. 141 | Jonesboro, AR 72401

Website: https://www.arkansasstateparks.com/parks/lake-frierson-state-park

Phone: 870-932-2615

Email: lakefrierson@arkansas.com

Established: 1975

Size: 114 acres (46.1 ha)

Star Rating ☆☆☆☆☆

What souvenir did you bring home?... _____

My favorite thing about this place is... _____

Why I went ... _____

Who I went with ... _____

When I went ... _____

What I did... _____

What I saw... _____

What I learned... _____

An unforgettable moment... _____

A laughable moment... _____

A surprising moment... _____

An unforeseeable moment... _____

My List

- ☐ _____
- ☐ _____
- ☐ _____
- ☐ _____
- ☐ _____
- ☐ _____
- ☐ _____
- ☐ _____
- ☐ _____
- ☐ _____
- ☐ _____

 Snapped a selfie | Location... _____

 Took a park sign selfie? - Y | N

The weather was ...

PLAN YOUR TRIP:

☐ Trip Plan Completed

☐ Day Trip   ☐ Overnight Stay

Reservations required: ☐ y ☐ n

Date reservations made: _____

Refund Policy: ☐ y ☐ n Site/Room #: _____

Confirmation #: _____

Miles to travel: _____

Time traveling: _____

Dog friendly?: ☐ y ☐ n

Activities Accomplished:

☐ Archery
☐ Biking
☐ Birding
☐ Boating
☐ Camping
☐ Caving
☐ Geocaching

☐ Fishing
☐ Hiking
☐ Horseback Riding
☐ Hunting
☐ Off-Roading
☐ Paddle Boarding
☐ Photography

☐ Picnicking
☐ Rock Climbing
☐ Shooting Range
☐ Snowshoeing
☐ Stargazing
☐ Swimming
☐ Tennis

☐ Walking
☐ Wildlife Watching
☐ _____
☐ _____
☐ _____
☐ _____
☐ _____

Traveled by:

☐ ☐ ☐ ☐ ☐ ☐ ☐ ☐ ☐ ☐ ☐ ☐

DESTINATION INFORMATION:

_____

PLACES WE DISCOVERED ALONG THE WAY

_____

_____

PLACES TO STOP AND SEE ALONG THE WAY

_____

_____

Would you go again?: ☐ y ☐ n   Open all year?: ☐ y ☐ n

Add your favorite ticket stub, postcard, photo, stamp or drawing here

NOT ALL THOSE WHO WANDER ARE LOST
N W E S

Lake Ouachita State Park

Address: 5451 Mountain Pine Rd | Mountain Pine, AR 71956

Website: https://www.arkansasstateparks.com/parks/lake-ouachita-state-park

Phone: 501-767-9366

Email: lakeouachita@arkansas.com

Established: 1955

Size: 360 acres (145.7 ha)

Star Rating
☆☆☆☆☆

What souvenir did you bring home?... _____

My favorite thing about this place is... _____

_____

Why I went ... _____

Who I went with ... _____

When I went ... _____

What I did... _____

What I saw... _____

_____

What I learned... _____

_____

An unforgettable moment... _____

_____

_____

A laughable moment... _____

_____

A surprising moment... _____

_____

_____

An unforeseeable moment... _____

_____

My List

- [ ] _____
- [ ] _____
- [ ] _____
- [ ] _____
- [ ] _____
- [ ] _____
- [ ] _____
- [ ] _____
- [ ] _____
- [ ] _____
- [ ] _____
- [ ] _____

Snapped a selfie | Location... _____

Took a park sign selfie? - Y | N   The weather was ...

PLAN YOUR TRIP:

DESTINATION INFORMATION:

☐ Trip Plan Completed

☐ Day Trip   ☐ Overnight Stay

Reservations required: ☐y ☐n

Date reservations made: _____

Refund Policy: ☐y ☐n Site/Room #: _____

Confirmation #: _____

Miles to travel: _____

Time traveling: _____

Dog friendly?: ☐y ☐n

_____

PLACES WE DISCOVERED ALONG THE WAY

_____
_____
_____

PLACES TO STOP AND SEE ALONG THE WAY

_____
_____
_____

Would you go again?: ☐y ☐n   Open all year?: ☐y ☐n

Activities Accomplished:

☐ Archery
☐ Biking
☐ Birding
☐ Boating
☐ Camping
☐ Caving
☐ Geocaching

☐ Fishing
☐ Hiking
☐ Horseback Riding
☐ Hunting
☐ Off-Roading
☐ Paddle Boarding
☐ Photography

☐ Picnicking
☐ Rock Climbing
☐ Shooting Range
☐ Snowshoeing
☐ Stargazing
☐ Swimming
☐ Tennis

☐ Walking
☐ Wildlife Watching
☐ _____
☐ _____
☐ _____
☐ _____
☐ _____

Traveled by:

☐ ☐ ☐ ☐ ☐ ☐ ☐ ☐ ☐ ☐ ☐ ☐

Add your favorite ticket stub, postcard, photo, stamp or drawing here

LET NEW ADVENTURES
»» BEGIN →

Lake Poinsett State Park

Address: 5752 State Park Lane | Harrisburg, AR 72432

Website: https://www.arkansasstateparks.com/parks/lake-poinsett-state-park

Phone: 870-578-2064

Email: lakepoinsett@arkansas.com

Established: 1963

Size: 132 acres (53.4 ha)

Star Rating
☆☆☆☆☆

What souvenir did you bring home?...

My favorite thing about this place is...

Why I went ...

Who I went with ...

When I went ...

What I did...

What I saw...

What I learned...

An unforgettable moment...

A laughable moment...

A surprising moment...

An unforeseeable moment...

My List
- [ ]
- [ ]
- [ ]
- [ ]
- [ ]
- [ ]
- [ ]
- [ ]
- [ ]
- [ ]
- [ ]

Snapped a selfie | Location...

Took a park sign selfie? - Y | N

The weather was ...

☐ Trip Plan Completed

☐ Day Trip   ☐ Overnight Stay

Reservations required: ☐y ☐n

Date reservations made: _____

Refund Policy: ☐y ☐n   Site/Room #: _____

Confirmation #: _____

Miles to travel: _____

Time traveling: _____

Dog friendly?: ☐y ☐n

PLACES WE DISCOVERED ALONG THE WAY

PLACES TO STOP AND SEE ALONG THE WAY

Would you go again?: ☐y ☐n   Open all year?: ☐y ☐n

Activities Accomplished:

☐ Archery
☐ Biking
☐ Birding
☐ Boating
☐ Camping
☐ Caving
☐ Geocaching

☐ Fishing
☐ Hiking
☐ Horseback Riding
☐ Hunting
☐ Off-Roading
☐ Paddle Boarding
☐ Photography

☐ Picnicking
☐ Rock Climbing
☐ Shooting Range
☐ Snowshoeing
☐ Stargazing
☐ Swimming
☐ Tennis

☐ Walking
☐ Wildlife Watching
☐ _____
☐ _____
☐ _____
☐ _____
☐ _____

Traveled by:

☐ ☐ ☐ ☐ ☐ ☐ ☐ ☐ ☐ ☐ ☐ ☐

Add your favorite ticket stub, postcard, photo, stamp or drawing here

NOT ALL THOSE WHO WANDER ARE LOST

N
W   E
S

Logoly State Park

Address: 131 Columbia Road 459 | Magnolia, AR 71753

Website: https://www.arkansasstateparks.com/parks/logoly-state-park

Phone: (870) 695-3561

Email: logoly@arkansas.com

Established: 1974

Size: 368 acres (148.9 ha)

Star Rating
☆☆☆☆☆

What souvenir did you bring home?...

My favorite thing about this place is...

Why I went ...

Who I went with ...

When I went ...

What I did...

What I saw...

What I learned...

An unforgettable moment...

A laughable moment...

A surprising moment...

An unforeseeable moment...

Snapped a selfie | Location...

Took a park sign selfie? - Y | N

The weather was ...

My List

- [ ]
- [ ]
- [ ]
- [ ]
- [ ]
- [ ]
- [ ]
- [ ]
- [ ]
- [ ]
- [ ]

PLAN YOUR TRIP:

DESTINATION INFORMATION:

☐ Trip Plan Completed

☐ Day Trip ☐ Overnight Stay

Reservations required: ☐y ☐n

Date reservations made: _____

Refund Policy: ☐y ☐n Site/Room #: _____

Confirmation #: _____

Miles to travel: _____

Time traveling: _____

Dog friendly?: ☐y ☐n

_____

PLACES WE DISCOVERED ALONG THE WAY

_____

_____

PLACES TO STOP AND SEE ALONG THE WAY

_____

_____

Would you go again?: ☐y ☐n   Open all year?: ☐y ☐n

Activities Accomplished:

☐ Archery
☐ Biking
☐ Birding
☐ Boating
☐ Camping
☐ Caving
☐ Geocaching

☐ Fishing
☐ Hiking
☐ Horseback Riding
☐ Hunting
☐ Off-Roading
☐ Paddle Boarding
☐ Photography

☐ Picnicking
☐ Rock Climbing
☐ Shooting Range
☐ Snowshoeing
☐ Stargazing
☐ Swimming
☐ Tennis

☐ Walking
☐ Wildlife Watching
☐ _____
☐ _____
☐ _____
☐ _____
☐ _____

Traveled by:

☐ ☐ ☐ ☐ ☐ ☐ ☐ ☐ ☐ ☐ ☐ ☐

Add your favorite ticket stub, postcard, photo, stamp or drawing here

LET NEW ADVENTURES
≫ BEGIN →

Louisiana Purchase State Park

Address: AR Hwy 362 | Brinkley, AR 72049

Website: https://www.arkansasstateparks.com/parks/louisiana-purchase-state-park

Phone: (501) 682-1191

Email: louisianapurchase@arkansas.com

Established: 1961

Size: 37.5 acres (15.2 ha)

What souvenir did you bring home?...

My favorite thing about this place is...

Star Rating
☆☆☆☆☆

Why I went ...

Who I went with ...

When I went ...

What I did...

What I saw...

What I learned...

An unforgettable moment...

A laughable moment...

A surprising moment...

An unforeseeable moment...

My List

- [ ]
- [ ]
- [ ]
- [ ]
- [ ]
- [ ]
- [ ]
- [ ]
- [ ]
- [ ]
- [ ]

Snapped a selfie | Location...

Took a park sign selfie? - Y | N

The weather was ...

PLAN YOUR TRIP:

☐ Trip Plan Completed

☐ Day Trip ☐ Overnight Stay

Reservations required: ☐y ☐n

Date reservations made: _____

Refund Policy: ☐y ☐n Site/Room #: _____

Confirmation #: _____

Miles to travel: _____

Time traveling: _____

Dog friendly?: ☐y ☐n

Activities Accomplished:

☐ Archery
☐ Biking
☐ Birding
☐ Boating
☐ Camping
☐ Caving
☐ Geocaching

☐ Fishing
☐ Hiking
☐ Horseback Riding
☐ Hunting
☐ Off-Roading
☐ Paddle Boarding
☐ Photography

☐ Picnicking
☐ Rock Climbing
☐ Shooting Range
☐ Snowshoeing
☐ Stargazing
☐ Swimming
☐ Tennis

☐ Walking
☐ Wildlife Watching
☐ _____
☐ _____
☐ _____
☐ _____
☐ _____

Traveled by:

☐ ☐ ☐ ☐ ☐ ☐ ☐ ☐ ☐ ☐ ☐ ☐

DESTINATION INFORMATION:

PLACES WE DISCOVERED ALONG THE WAY

PLACES TO STOP AND SEE ALONG THE WAY

Would you go again?: ☐y ☐n   Open all year?: ☐y ☐n

Add your favorite ticket stub, postcard, photo, stamp or drawing here

NOT ALL THOSE WHO WANDER ARE LOST

Lower White River Museum State Park

Address: 2009 Main Street | Des Arc, AR 72040

Website: https://www.arkansasstateparks.com/parks/lower-white-river-museum-state-park

Phone: 870-256-3711

Email: lowerwhiterivermuseum@arkansas.com

Established: 1975

Size: 0.4 acres (0.2 ha)

What souvenir did you bring home?... _____

My favorite thing about this place is... _____

Star Rating
☆ ☆ ☆ ☆ ☆

Why I went ... _____

Who I went with ... _____

When I went ... _____

What I did... _____

What I saw... _____

What I learned... _____

An unforgettable moment... _____

A laughable moment... _____

A surprising moment... _____

An unforeseeable moment... _____

My List
- ☐ _____
- ☐ _____
- ☐ _____
- ☐ _____
- ☐ _____
- ☐ _____
- ☐ _____
- ☐ _____
- ☐ _____
- ☐ _____
- ☐ _____
- ☐ _____

Snapped a selfie | Location... _____

Took a park sign selfie? - Y | N   The weather was ...

DESTINATION INFORMATION:

☐ Trip Plan Completed

☐ Day Trip ☐ Overnight Stay

Reservations required: ☐y ☐n

Date reservations made: _____

Refund Policy: ☐y ☐n Site/Room #: _____

Confirmation #: _____

Miles to travel: _____

Time traveling: _____

Dog friendly?: ☐y ☐n

PLACES WE DISCOVERED ALONG THE WAY

PLACES TO STOP AND SEE ALONG THE WAY

Would you go again?: ☐y ☐n   Open all year?: ☐y ☐n

Activities Accomplished:

☐ Archery
☐ Biking
☐ Birding
☐ Boating
☐ Camping
☐ Caving
☐ Geocaching

☐ Fishing
☐ Hiking
☐ Horseback Riding
☐ Hunting
☐ Off-Roading
☐ Paddle Boarding
☐ Photography

☐ Picnicking
☐ Rock Climbing
☐ Shooting Range
☐ Snowshoeing
☐ Stargazing
☐ Swimming
☐ Tennis

☐ Walking
☐ Wildlife Watching
☐ _____
☐ _____
☐ _____
☐ _____
☐ _____

Traveled by:

☐ ☐ ☐ ☐ ☐ ☐ ☐ ☐ ☐ ☐ ☐ ☐

Add your favorite ticket stub, postcard, photo, stamp or drawing here

LET NEW ADVENTURES
»> BEGIN →

Mammoth Spring State Park

Address: 17 US Hwy 63, Mammoth Spring, AR 72554

Website: https://www.arkansasstateparks.com/parks/mammoth-spring-state-park

Phone: 870-625-7364

Email: mammothspring@arkansas.com

Established: 1957

Size: 623.5 acres (25 ha)

Star Rating
☆ ☆ ☆ ☆ ☆

What souvenir did you bring home?... _____

My favorite thing about this place is... _____

Why I went ... _____

Who I went with ... _____

When I went ... _____

What I did... _____

What I saw... _____

What I learned... _____

An unforgettable moment... _____

A laughable moment... _____

A surprising moment... _____

An unforeseeable moment... _____

My List
- ☐ _____
- ☐ _____
- ☐ _____
- ☐ _____
- ☐ _____
- ☐ _____
- ☐ _____
- ☐ _____
- ☐ _____
- ☐ _____
- ☐ _____

Snapped a selfie | Location... _____

Took a park sign selfie? - Y | N   The weather was ...

PLAN YOUR TRIP:

- ☐ Trip Plan Completed
- ☐ Day Trip   ☐ Overnight Stay

Reservations required: ☐y ☐n

Date reservations made: _____

Refund Policy: ☐y ☐n Site/Room #: _____

Confirmation #: _____

Miles to travel: _____

Time traveling: _____

Dog friendly?: ☐y ☐n

Activities Accomplished:

- ☐ Archery
- ☐ Biking
- ☐ Birding
- ☐ Boating
- ☐ Camping
- ☐ Caving
- ☐ Geocaching
- ☐ Fishing
- ☐ Hiking
- ☐ Horseback Riding
- ☐ Hunting
- ☐ Off-Roading
- ☐ Paddle Boarding
- ☐ Photography
- ☐ Picnicking
- ☐ Rock Climbing
- ☐ Shooting Range
- ☐ Snowshoeing
- ☐ Stargazing
- ☐ Swimming
- ☐ Tennis
- ☐ Walking
- ☐ Wildlife Watching
- ☐ _____
- ☐ _____
- ☐ _____
- ☐ _____
- ☐ _____

Traveled by:

☐ ☐ ☐ ☐ ☐ ☐ ☐ ☐ ☐ ☐ ☐ ☐

DESTINATION INFORMATION:

_____

PLACES WE DISCOVERED ALONG THE WAY

_____

PLACES TO STOP AND SEE ALONG THE WAY

_____

Would you go again? ☐y ☐n   Open all year? ☐y ☐n

Add your favorite ticket stub, postcard, photo, stamp or drawing here

NOT ALL THOSE WHO WANDER ARE LOST

N W E S

Marks' Mills Battleground State Park

Address: Ark Hwy 8 | Fordyce, AR 71660

Website: https://www.arkansasstateparks.com/parks/marks-mills-battleground-state-park

Phone: 888-287-2757

Email: marksmills@arkansas.com

Established: 1961

Size: 6.2 acres (2.5 ha)

Star Rating
☆☆☆☆☆

What souvenir did you bring home?...

My favorite thing about this place is...

Why I went ...

Who I went with ...

When I went ...

What I did...

What I saw...

What I learned...

An unforgettable moment...

A laughable moment...

A surprising moment...

An unforeseeable moment...

My List

- ☐
- ☐
- ☐
- ☐
- ☐
- ☐
- ☐
- ☐
- ☐
- ☐
- ☐

Snapped a selfie | Location...

Took a park sign selfie? - Y | N   The weather was ...

PLAN YOUR TRIP:

☐ Trip Plan Completed

☐ Day Trip   ☐ Overnight Stay

Reservations required: ☐ y ☐ n

Date reservations made: _____

Refund Policy: ☐ y ☐ n   Site/Room #: _____

Confirmation #: _____

Miles to travel: _____

Time traveling: _____

Dog friendly?: ☐ y ☐ n

Activities Accomplished:

☐ Archery
☐ Biking
☐ Birding
☐ Boating
☐ Camping
☐ Caving
☐ Geocaching

☐ Fishing
☐ Hiking
☐ Horseback Riding
☐ Hunting
☐ Off-Roading
☐ Paddle Boarding
☐ Photography

☐ Picnicking
☐ Rock Climbing
☐ Shooting Range
☐ Snowshoeing
☐ Stargazing
☐ Swimming
☐ Tennis

☐ Walking
☐ Wildlife Watching
☐ _____
☐ _____
☐ _____
☐ _____
☐ _____

DESTINATION INFORMATION:

_____

PLACES WE DISCOVERED ALONG THE WAY

_____
_____
_____

PLACES TO STOP AND SEE ALONG THE WAY

_____
_____
_____

Would you go again? ☐ y ☐ n   Open all year? ☐ y ☐ n

Traveled by:

☐ ☐ ☐ ☐ ☐ ☐ ☐ ☐ ☐ ☐ ☐ ☐

Add your favorite ticket stub, postcard, photo, stamp or drawing here

LET NEW ADVENTURES
»» BEGIN →

MILLWOOD STATE PARK

Address: 1564 Hwy. 32 East | Ashdown, AR 71822

Website: https://www.arkansasstateparks.com/parks/millwood-state-park

Phone: 870-898-2800

Email: millwood@arkansas.com

Established: 1976

Size: 824 acres (333 ha)

What souvenir did you bring home?...

My favorite thing about this place is...

Star Rating
☆☆☆☆☆

Why I went ...

Who I went with ...

When I went ...

What I did...

What I saw...

What I learned...

An unforgettable moment...

A laughable moment...

A surprising moment...

My List

- ☐
- ☐
- ☐
- ☐
- ☐
- ☐
- ☐
- ☐
- ☐
- ☐
- ☐

An unforeseeable moment...

Snapped a selfie | Location...

Took a park sign selfie? - Y | N   The weather was ...

☐ Trip Plan Completed

☐ Day Trip   ☐ Overnight Stay

Reservations required: ☐ y ☐ n

Date reservations made: _____

Refund Policy: ☐ y ☐ n Site/Room #: _____

Confirmation #: _____

Miles to travel: _____

Time traveling: _____

Dog friendly?: ☐ y ☐ n

PLACES WE DISCOVERED ALONG THE WAY

PLACES TO STOP AND SEE ALONG THE WAY

Would you go again? ☐ y ☐ n   Open all year? ☐ y ☐ n

Activities Accomplished:

☐ Archery
☐ Biking
☐ Birding
☐ Boating
☐ Camping
☐ Caving
☐ Geocaching

☐ Fishing
☐ Hiking
☐ Horseback Riding
☐ Hunting
☐ Off-Roading
☐ Paddle Boarding
☐ Photography

☐ Picnicking
☐ Rock Climbing
☐ Shooting Range
☐ Snowshoeing
☐ Stargazing
☐ Swimming
☐ Tennis

☐ Walking
☐ Wildlife Watching
☐ _____
☐ _____
☐ _____
☐ _____
☐ _____

Traveled by:

☐ ☐ ☐ ☐ ☐ ☐ ☐ ☐ ☐ ☐ ☐ ☐

Add your favorite ticket stub, postcard, photo, stamp or drawing here

NOT ALL THOSE WHO WANDER ARE LOST

N
W   E
S

Mississippi River State Park

Address: 2955 Hwy. 44 | Marianna, AR 72360

Website: https://www.arkansasstateparks.com/parks/mississippi-river-state-park

Phone: 870-295-4040

Email: mississippiriver@arkansas.com

Established: 2009

Size: 536 acres (217 ha)

Star Rating
☆☆☆☆☆

What souvenir did you bring home?... _____

My favorite thing about this place is... _____

Why I went ... _____

Who I went with ... _____

When I went ... _____

What I did... _____

What I saw... _____

What I learned... _____

An unforgettable moment... _____

A laughable moment... _____

A surprising moment... _____

My List

- ☐ _____
- ☐ _____
- ☐ _____
- ☐ _____
- ☐ _____
- ☐ _____
- ☐ _____
- ☐ _____
- ☐ _____
- ☐ _____
- ☐ _____

An unforeseeable moment... _____

Snapped a selfie | Location... _____

Took a park sign selfie? - Y | N   The weather was ...

PLAN YOUR TRIP:

DESTINATION INFORMATION:

☐ Trip Plan Completed

☐ Day Trip   ☐ Overnight Stay

Reservations required: ☐y ☐n

Date reservations made: _____

Refund Policy: ☐y ☐n Site/Room #: _____

Confirmation #: _____

Miles to travel: _____

Time traveling: _____

Dog friendly?: ☐y ☐n

PLACES WE DISCOVERED ALONG THE WAY

_____

_____

PLACES TO STOP AND SEE ALONG THE WAY

_____

_____

Would you go again?: ☐y ☐n   Open all year?: ☐y ☐n

Activities Accomplished:

☐ Archery
☐ Biking
☐ Birding
☐ Boating
☐ Camping
☐ Caving
☐ Geocaching

☐ Fishing
☐ Hiking
☐ Horseback Riding
☐ Hunting
☐ Off-Roading
☐ Paddle Boarding
☐ Photography

☐ Picnicking
☐ Rock Climbing
☐ Shooting Range
☐ Snowshoeing
☐ Stargazing
☐ Swimming
☐ Tennis

☐ Walking
☐ Wildlife Watching
☐ _____
☐ _____
☐ _____
☐ _____
☐ _____

Traveled by:

☐ ☐ ☐ ☐ ☐ ☐ ☐ ☐ ☐ ☐ ☐ ☐

Add your favorite ticket stub, postcard, photo, stamp or drawing here

LET NEW ADVENTURES
≫ BEGIN →

Moro Bay State Park

Address: 6071 Hwy. 600 | Jersey, AR 71651

Website: https://www.arkansasstateparks.com/parks/moro-bay-state-park

Phone: 870-463-8555

Email: morobay@arkansas.com

Established: 1972

Size: 117 acres (47 ha)

Star Rating
☆☆☆☆☆

What souvenir did you bring home?... _____

My favorite thing about this place is... _____

Why I went ... _____

Who I went with ... _____

When I went ... _____

What I did... _____

What I saw... _____

What I learned... _____

An unforgettable moment... _____

A laughable moment... _____

A surprising moment... _____

An unforeseeable moment... _____

Snapped a selfie | Location... _____

Took a park sign selfie? - Y | N

The weather was ...

My List
- ☐ _____
- ☐ _____
- ☐ _____
- ☐ _____
- ☐ _____
- ☐ _____
- ☐ _____
- ☐ _____
- ☐ _____
- ☐ _____
- ☐ _____

PLAN YOUR TRIP:

- ☐ Trip Plan Completed
- ☐ Day Trip ☐ Overnight Stay

Reservations required: ☐y ☐n

Date reservations made: _____

Refund Policy: ☐y ☐n Site/Room #: _____

Confirmation #: _____

Miles to travel: _____

Time traveling: _____

Dog friendly?: ☐y ☐n

Activities Accomplished:

- ☐ Archery
- ☐ Biking
- ☐ Birding
- ☐ Boating
- ☐ Camping
- ☐ Caving
- ☐ Geocaching
- ☐ Fishing
- ☐ Hiking
- ☐ Horseback Riding
- ☐ Hunting
- ☐ Off-Roading
- ☐ Paddle Boarding
- ☐ Photography
- ☐ Picnicking
- ☐ Rock Climbing
- ☐ Shooting Range
- ☐ Snowshoeing
- ☐ Stargazing
- ☐ Swimming
- ☐ Tennis
- ☐ Walking
- ☐ Wildlife Watching
- ☐ _____
- ☐ _____
- ☐ _____
- ☐ _____
- ☐ _____

Traveled by:

☐ ☐ ☐ ☐ ☐ ☐ ☐ ☐ ☐ ☐ ☐ ☐

DESTINATION INFORMATION:

PLACES WE DISCOVERED ALONG THE WAY

PLACES TO STOP AND SEE ALONG THE WAY

Would you go again?: ☐y ☐n Open all year?: ☐y ☐n

Add your favorite ticket stub, postcard, photo, stamp or drawing here

NOT ALL THOSE WHO WANDER ARE LOST

Mount Magazine State Park

Address: 16878 AR-309 | Paris, AR 72855

Website: https://www.arkansasstateparks.com/parks/mount-magazine-state-park

Phone: 479-963-8502

Email: mountmagazine@arkansas.com

Established: 1983

Size: 2,234 acres (904 ha)

Star Rating
☆☆☆☆☆

What souvenir did you bring home?...

My favorite thing about this place is...

Why I went ...

Who I went with ...

When I went ...

What I did...

What I saw...

What I learned...

An unforgettable moment...

A laughable moment...

A surprising moment...

An unforeseeable moment...

My List

- [ ]
- [ ]
- [ ]
- [ ]
- [ ]
- [ ]
- [ ]
- [ ]
- [ ]
- [ ]
- [ ]

Snapped a selfie | Location...

Took a park sign selfie? - Y | N

The weather was ...

PLAN YOUR TRIP:

- ☐ Trip Plan Completed
- ☐ Day Trip   ☐ Overnight Stay

Reservations required: ☐ y ☐ n

Date reservations made: _____

Refund Policy: ☐ y ☐ n Site/Room #: _____

Confirmation #: _____

Miles to travel: _____

Time traveling: _____

Dog friendly?: ☐ y ☐ n

Activities Accomplished:

☐ Archery	☐ Fishing	☐ Picnicking	☐ Walking
☐ Biking	☐ Hiking	☐ Rock Climbing	☐ Wildlife Watching
☐ Birding	☐ Horseback Riding	☐ Shooting Range	☐ _____
☐ Boating	☐ Hunting	☐ Snowshoeing	☐ _____
☐ Camping	☐ Off-Roading	☐ Stargazing	☐ _____
☐ Caving	☐ Paddle Boarding	☐ Swimming	☐ _____
☐ Geocaching	☐ Photography	☐ Tennis	☐ _____

Traveled by:

☐ ☐ ☐ ☐ ☐ ☐ ☐ ☐ ☐ ☐ ☐ ☐

DESTINATION INFORMATION:

_____
_____

PLACES WE DISCOVERED ALONG THE WAY

_____
_____
_____

PLACES TO STOP AND SEE ALONG THE WAY

_____
_____
_____

Would you go again? ☐ y ☐ n   Open all year?: ☐ y ☐ n

Add your favorite ticket stub, postcard, photo, stamp or drawing here

LET NEW ADVENTURES
»» BEGIN →

Mount Nebo State Park

Address: 16728 West State Hwy. 155 | Dardanelle, AR 72834

Website: https://www.arkansasstateparks.com/parks/mount-nebo-state-park

Phone: 479-229-3655

Email: mountnebo@arkansas.com

Established: 1928

Size: 2,984 acres (1208 ha)

Star Rating
☆☆☆☆☆

What souvenir did you bring home?... _____

My favorite thing about this place is... _____

Why I went ... _____

Who I went with ... _____

When I went ... _____

What I did... _____

What I saw... _____

What I learned... _____

An unforgettable moment... _____

A laughable moment... _____

A surprising moment... _____

An unforeseeable moment... _____

My List

- [ ] _____
- [ ] _____
- [ ] _____
- [ ] _____
- [ ] _____
- [ ] _____
- [ ] _____
- [ ] _____
- [ ] _____
- [ ] _____
- [ ] _____

Snapped a selfie | Location... _____

Took a park sign selfie? - Y | N

The weather was ...

☐ Trip Plan Completed

☐ Day Trip   ☐ Overnight Stay

Reservations required: ☐y ☐n

Date reservations made: _____

Refund Policy: ☐y ☐n Site/Room #: _____

Confirmation #: _____

Miles to travel: _____

Time traveling: _____

Dog friendly?: ☐y ☐n

PLACES WE DISCOVERED ALONG THE WAY

_____

_____

PLACES TO STOP AND SEE ALONG THE WAY

_____

_____

Activities Accomplished:

Would you go again?: ☐y ☐n   Open all year?: ☐y ☐n

☐ Archery
☐ Biking
☐ Birding
☐ Boating
☐ Camping
☐ Caving
☐ Geocaching

☐ Fishing
☐ Hiking
☐ Horseback Riding
☐ Hunting
☐ Off-Roading
☐ Paddle Boarding
☐ Photography

☐ Picnicking
☐ Rock Climbing
☐ Shooting Range
☐ Snowshoeing
☐ Stargazing
☐ Swimming
☐ Tennis

☐ Walking
☐ Wildlife Watching
☐ _____
☐ _____
☐ _____
☐ _____
☐ _____

Traveled by:

☐ ☐ ☐ ☐ ☐ ☐ ☐ ☐ ☐ ☐ ☐ ☐

Add your favorite ticket stub, postcard, photo, stamp or drawing here

N
NOT ALL THOSE WHO
W   E
WANDER ARE LOST
S

Ozark Folk Center State Park

Address: 1032 Park Avenue | Mountain View, AR 72560

Website: https://www.arkansasstateparks.com/parks/ozark-folk-center-state-park

Phone: 870-269-3851

Email: ozarkfolkcenter@arkansas.com

Established: 1973

Size: 637 acres (258 ha)

Star Rating
☆☆☆☆☆

What souvenir did you bring home?... _____

My favorite thing about this place is... _____

Why I went ... _____

Who I went with ... _____

When I went ... _____

What I did... _____

What I saw... _____

What I learned... _____

An unforgettable moment... _____

A laughable moment... _____

A surprising moment... _____

An unforeseeable moment... _____

My List

- ☐ _____
- ☐ _____
- ☐ _____
- ☐ _____
- ☐ _____
- ☐ _____
- ☐ _____
- ☐ _____
- ☐ _____
- ☐ _____
- ☐ _____
- ☐ _____

Snapped a selfie | Location... _____

Took a park sign selfie? - y | n

The weather was ...

PLAN YOUR TRIP:

☐ Trip Plan Completed
☐ Day Trip ☐ Overnight Stay
Reservations required: ☐y ☐n
Date reservations made: _____
Refund Policy: ☐y ☐n Site/Room #: _____
Confirmation #: _____
Miles to travel: _____
Time traveling: _____
Dog friendly?: ☐y ☐n

Activities Accomplished:

☐ Archery
☐ Biking
☐ Birding
☐ Boating
☐ Camping
☐ Caving
☐ Geocaching

☐ Fishing
☐ Hiking
☐ Horseback Riding
☐ Hunting
☐ Off-Roading
☐ Paddle Boarding
☐ Photography

☐ Picnicking
☐ Rock Climbing
☐ Shooting Range
☐ Snowshoeing
☐ Stargazing
☐ Swimming
☐ Tennis

☐ Walking
☐ Wildlife Watching
☐ _____
☐ _____
☐ _____
☐ _____
☐ _____

DESTINATION INFORMATION:

_____
_____

PLACES WE DISCOVERED ALONG THE WAY

_____
_____
_____

PLACES TO STOP AND SEE ALONG THE WAY

_____
_____
_____

Would you go again?: ☐y ☐n   Open all year?: ☐y ☐n

Traveled by:

☐ ☐ ☐ ☐ ☐ ☐ ☐ ☐ ☐ ☐ ☐ ☐

Add your favorite ticket stub, postcard, photo, stamp or drawing here

LET NEW ADVENTURES
>> BEGIN →

PARKIN ARCHEOLOGICAL STATE PARK

Address: 60 State Hwy 184 | Parkin, AR 72373

Website: https://www.arkansasstateparks.com/parks/parkin-archeological-state-park

Phone: 870-755-2500

Email: parkin@arkansas.com

Established: 1994

Size: 107 acres (43 ha)

What souvenir did you bring home?... _____

My favorite thing about this place is... _____

Star Rating
☆☆☆☆☆

Why I went ... _____

Who I went with ... _____

When I went ... _____

What I did... _____

What I saw... _____

What I learned... _____

An unforgettable moment... _____

A laughable moment... _____

A surprising moment... _____

An unforeseeable moment... _____

My List

- ☐ _____
- ☐ _____
- ☐ _____
- ☐ _____
- ☐ _____
- ☐ _____
- ☐ _____
- ☐ _____
- ☐ _____
- ☐ _____
- ☐ _____
- ☐ _____

Snapped a selfie | Location... _____

Took a park sign selfie? - Y | N   The weather was ...

PLAN YOUR TRIP:

☐ Trip Plan Completed

☐ Day Trip   ☐ Overnight Stay

Reservations required: ☐y ☐n

Date reservations made: _____

Refund Policy: ☐y ☐n Site/Room #: _____

Confirmation #: _____

Miles to travel: _____

Time traveling: _____

Dog friendly?: ☐y ☐n

Activities Accomplished:

☐ Archery
☐ Biking
☐ Birding
☐ Boating
☐ Camping
☐ Caving
☐ Geocaching

☐ Fishing
☐ Hiking
☐ Horseback Riding
☐ Hunting
☐ Off-Roading
☐ Paddle Boarding
☐ Photography

☐ Picnicking
☐ Rock Climbing
☐ Shooting Range
☐ Snowshoeing
☐ Stargazing
☐ Swimming
☐ Tennis

☐ Walking
☐ Wildlife Watching
☐ _____
☐ _____
☐ _____
☐ _____
☐ _____

Traveled by:

☐ ☐ ☐ ☐ ☐ ☐ ☐ ☐ ☐ ☐ ☐ ☐

DESTINATION INFORMATION:

_____
_____

PLACES WE DISCOVERED ALONG THE WAY

_____
_____
_____

PLACES TO STOP AND SEE ALONG THE WAY

_____
_____
_____

Would you go again? ☐y ☐n   Open all year? ☐y ☐n

Add your favorite ticket stub, postcard, photo, stamp or drawing here

Petit Jean State Park

Address: 1285 Petit Jean Mountain Road | Morrilton, AR 72110

Website: https://www.arkansasstateparks.com/parks/petit-jean-state-park

Phone: 501-727-5441

Email: petitjean@arkansas.com

Established: 1923

Size: 3,471 acres (1405 ha)

Star Rating
☆☆☆☆☆

What souvenir did you bring home?... _____

My favorite thing about this place is... _____

Why I went ... _____

Who I went with ... _____

When I went ... _____

What I did... _____

What I saw... _____

What I learned... _____

An unforgettable moment... _____

A laughable moment... _____

A surprising moment... _____

An unforeseeable moment... _____

My List
- [ ] _____
- [ ] _____
- [ ] _____
- [ ] _____
- [ ] _____
- [ ] _____
- [ ] _____
- [ ] _____
- [ ] _____
- [ ] _____
- [ ] _____

Snapped a selfie | Location... _____

Took a park sign selfie? - Y | N

The weather was ...

PLAN YOUR TRIP:

DESTINATION INFORMATION:

☐ Trip Plan Completed

☐ Day Trip   ☐ Overnight Stay

Reservations required: ☐ y ☐ n

Date reservations made: _____

Refund Policy: ☐ y ☐ n Site/Room #: _____

Confirmation #: _____

Miles to travel: _____

Time traveling: _____

Dog friendly?: ☐ y ☐ n

PLACES WE DISCOVERED ALONG THE WAY

PLACES TO STOP AND SEE ALONG THE WAY

Would you go again?: ☐ y ☐ n   Open all year?: ☐ y ☐ n

Activities Accomplished:

☐ Archery
☐ Biking
☐ Birding
☐ Boating
☐ Camping
☐ Caving
☐ Geocaching

☐ Fishing
☐ Hiking
☐ Horseback Riding
☐ Hunting
☐ Off-Roading
☐ Paddle Boarding
☐ Photography

☐ Picnicking
☐ Rock Climbing
☐ Shooting Range
☐ Snowshoeing
☐ Stargazing
☐ Swimming
☐ Tennis

☐ Walking
☐ Wildlife Watching
☐ _____
☐ _____
☐ _____
☐ _____
☐ _____

Traveled by:

☐ ☐ ☐ ☐ ☐ ☐ ☐ ☐ ☐ ☐ ☐ ☐

Add your favorite ticket stub, postcard, photo, stamp or drawing here

LET NEW ADVENTURES
» BEGIN →

PINNACLE MOUNTAIN STATE PARK

Address: 11901 Pinnacle Valley Road | Little Rock, AR 72223

Website: https://www.arkansasstateparks.com/parks/pinnacle-mountain-state-park

Phone: 501-868-5806

Email: pinnaclemountain@arkansas.com

Established: 1973

Size: 2,069 acres (837 ha)

What souvenir did you bring home?...

My favorite thing about this place is...

Star Rating
☆☆☆☆☆

Why I went ...

Who I went with ...

When I went ...

What I did...

What I saw...

What I learned...

An unforgettable moment...

A laughable moment...

A surprising moment...

An unforeseeable moment...

My List
- ☐
- ☐
- ☐
- ☐
- ☐
- ☐
- ☐
- ☐
- ☐
- ☐
- ☐
- ☐

Snapped a selfie | Location...

Took a park sign selfie? - y | n   The weather was ...

www.mynaturebookadventures.com

93

PLAN YOUR TRIP:

DESTINATION INFORMATION:

☐ Trip Plan Completed

☐ Day Trip   ☐ Overnight Stay

Reservations required: ☐ y ☐ n

Date reservations made: _____

Refund Policy: ☐ y ☐ n Site/Room #: _____

Confirmation #: _____

Miles to travel: _____

Time traveling: _____

Dog friendly?: ☐ y ☐ n

PLACES WE DISCOVERED ALONG THE WAY

PLACES TO STOP AND SEE ALONG THE WAY

Would you go again?: ☐ y ☐ n   Open all year?: ☐ y ☐ n

Activities Accomplished:

☐ Archery
☐ Biking
☐ Birding
☐ Boating
☐ Camping
☐ Caving
☐ Geocaching

☐ Fishing
☐ Hiking
☐ Horseback Riding
☐ Hunting
☐ Off-Roading
☐ Paddle Boarding
☐ Photography

☐ Picnicking
☐ Rock Climbing
☐ Shooting Range
☐ Snowshoeing
☐ Stargazing
☐ Swimming
☐ Tennis

☐ Walking
☐ Wildlife Watching
☐ _____
☐ _____
☐ _____
☐ _____
☐ _____

Traveled by:

☐ ☐ ☐ ☐ ☐ ☐ ☐ ☐ ☐ ☐ ☐ ☐

Add your favorite ticket stub, postcard, photo, stamp or drawing here

Plantation Agriculture Museum

Address: 4815 AR Hwy 161 South | Scott, AR 72142

Website: https://www.arkansasstateparks.com/parks/plantation-agriculture-museum

Phone: 501-961-1409

Email: plantationagrimuseum@arkansas.com

Established: 1985

Size: 14.5 acres (5.9 ha)

Star Rating
☆☆☆☆☆

What souvenir did you bring home?...

My favorite thing about this place is...

Why I went ...

Who I went with ...

When I went ...

What I did...

What I saw...

What I learned...

An unforgettable moment...

A laughable moment...

A surprising moment...

An unforeseeable moment...

My List

- [ ]
- [ ]
- [ ]
- [ ]
- [ ]
- [ ]
- [ ]
- [ ]
- [ ]
- [ ]
- [ ]

Snapped a selfie | Location...

Took a park sign selfie? - y | n

The weather was ...

☐ Trip Plan Completed

☐ Day Trip　　☐ Overnight Stay

Reservations required: ☐y ☐n

Date reservations made: _____

Refund Policy: ☐y ☐n Site/Room #: _____

Confirmation #: _____

Miles to travel: _____

Time traveling: _____

Dog friendly?: ☐y ☐n

PLACES WE DISCOVERED ALONG THE WAY

PLACES TO STOP AND SEE ALONG THE WAY

Would you go again?: ☐y ☐n   Open all year?: ☐y ☐n

Activities Accomplished:

☐ Archery
☐ Biking
☐ Birding
☐ Boating
☐ Camping
☐ Caving
☐ Geocaching

☐ Fishing
☐ Hiking
☐ Horseback Riding
☐ Hunting
☐ Off-Roading
☐ Paddle Boarding
☐ Photography

☐ Picnicking
☐ Rock Climbing
☐ Shooting Range
☐ Snowshoeing
☐ Stargazing
☐ Swimming
☐ Tennis

☐ Walking
☐ Wildlife Watching
☐ _____
☐ _____
☐ _____
☐ _____
☐ _____

Traveled by:

☐ ☐ ☐ ☐ ☐ ☐ ☐ ☐ ☐ ☐ ☐ ☐

Add your favorite ticket stub, postcard, photo, stamp or drawing here

LET NEW ADVENTURES
>> BEGIN →

Poison Springs Battleground State Park

Address: Ark Hwy 76 | Camden, AR 71722

Website: https://www.arkansasstateparks.com/parks/poison-springs-battleground-state-park

Phone: 888-287-2757

Email: poisonspring@arkansas.com

Established: 1961

Size: 85 acres (34 ha)

What souvenir did you bring home?...

My favorite thing about this place is...

Star Rating
☆☆☆☆☆

Why I went ...

Who I went with ...

When I went ...

What I did...

What I saw...

What I learned...

An unforgettable moment...

A laughable moment...

A surprising moment...

An unforeseeable moment...

My List

- ☐
- ☐
- ☐
- ☐
- ☐
- ☐
- ☐
- ☐
- ☐
- ☐
- ☐
- ☐

Snapped a selfie | Location...

Took a park sign selfie? - Y | N

The weather was ...

PLAN YOUR TRIP:

DESTINATION INFORMATION:

☐ Trip Plan Completed

☐ Day Trip ☐ Overnight Stay

Reservations required: ☐y ☐n

Date reservations made: _____

Refund Policy: ☐y ☐n Site/Room #: _____

Confirmation #: _____

Miles to travel: _____

Time traveling: _____

Dog friendly?: ☐y ☐n

PLACES WE DISCOVERED ALONG THE WAY

_____

_____

PLACES TO STOP AND SEE ALONG THE WAY

_____

_____

Would you go again? ☐y ☐n   Open all year? ☐y ☐n

Activities Accomplished:

☐ Archery
☐ Biking
☐ Birding
☐ Boating
☐ Camping
☐ Caving
☐ Geocaching

☐ Fishing
☐ Hiking
☐ Horseback Riding
☐ Hunting
☐ Off-Roading
☐ Paddle Boarding
☐ Photography

☐ Picnicking
☐ Rock Climbing
☐ Shooting Range
☐ Snowshoeing
☐ Stargazing
☐ Swimming
☐ Tennis

☐ Walking
☐ Wildlife Watching
☐ _____
☐ _____
☐ _____
☐ _____
☐ _____

Traveled by:

☐ ☐ ☐ ☐ ☐ ☐ ☐ ☐ ☐ ☐ ☐ ☐

Add your favorite ticket stub, postcard, photo, stamp or drawing here

N E S W — NOT ALL THOSE WHO WANDER ARE LOST

Powhatan Historic State Park

Address: 4414 Hwy 25 | Powhatan, AR 72458

Website: https://www.arkansasstateparks.com/parks/powhatan-historic-state-park

Phone: 870-878-6765

Email: powhatan@arkansas.com

Established: 1970

Size: 9.1 acres (3.7 ha)

Star Rating
☆☆☆☆☆

What souvenir did you bring home?...

My favorite thing about this place is...

Why I went ...

Who I went with ...

When I went ...

What I did...

What I saw...

What I learned...

An unforgettable moment...

A laughable moment...

A surprising moment...

An unforeseeable moment...

My List

- [ ]
- [ ]
- [ ]
- [ ]
- [ ]
- [ ]
- [ ]
- [ ]
- [ ]
- [ ]
- [ ]

Snapped a selfie | Location...

Took a park sign selfie? - Y | N

The weather was ...

Destination Information:

☐ Trip Plan Completed
☐ Day Trip   ☐ Overnight Stay
Reservations required: ☐ y ☐ n
Date reservations made: _____
Refund Policy: ☐ y ☐ n Site/Room #: _____
Confirmation #: _____
Miles to travel: _____
Time traveling: _____
Dog friendly?: ☐ y ☐ n

_____

Places We Discovered Along The Way
_____
_____

Places To Stop And See Along The Way
_____
_____

Activities Accomplished:

Would you go again?: ☐ y ☐ n   Open all year?: ☐ y ☐ n

☐ Archery	☐ Fishing	☐ Picnicking	☐ Walking
☐ Biking	☐ Hiking	☐ Rock Climbing	☐ Wildlife Watching
☐ Birding	☐ Horseback Riding	☐ Shooting Range	☐ _____
☐ Boating	☐ Hunting	☐ Snowshoeing	☐ _____
☐ Camping	☐ Off-Roading	☐ Stargazing	☐ _____
☐ Caving	☐ Paddle Boarding	☐ Swimming	☐ _____
☐ Geocaching	☐ Photography	☐ Tennis	☐ _____

Traveled by:

☐ ☐ ☐ ☐ ☐ ☐ ☐ ☐ ☐ ☐ ☐ ☐

Add your favorite ticket stub, postcard, photo, stamp or drawing here

LET NEW ADVENTURES
» BEGIN →

Prairie Grove Battlefield State Park

Address: 506 East Douglas Street | Prairie Grove, AR 72753

Website: https://www.arkansasstateparks.com/parks/prairie-grove-battlefield-state-park

Phone: 479-846-2990

Email: prairiegrove@arkansas.com

Established: 1957

Size: 840 acres (340 ha)

Star Rating
☆☆☆☆☆

What souvenir did you bring home?...

My favorite thing about this place is...

Why I went ...

Who I went with ...

When I went ...

What I did...

What I saw...

What I learned...

An unforgettable moment...

A laughable moment...

A surprising moment...

An unforeseeable moment...

My List
- [ ]
- [ ]
- [ ]
- [ ]
- [ ]
- [ ]
- [ ]
- [ ]
- [ ]
- [ ]
- [ ]

Snapped a selfie | Location...

Took a park sign selfie? - Y | N

The weather was ...

PLAN YOUR TRIP:

DESTINATION INFORMATION:

- ☐ Trip Plan Completed
- ☐ Day Trip   ☐ Overnight Stay

Reservations required: ☐y ☐n

Date reservations made: _____

Refund Policy: ☐y ☐n Site/Room #: _____

Confirmation #: _____

Miles to travel: _____

Time traveling: _____

Dog friendly?: ☐y ☐n

PLACES WE DISCOVERED ALONG THE WAY

PLACES TO STOP AND SEE ALONG THE WAY

Would you go again?: ☐y ☐n   Open all year?: ☐y ☐n

Activities Accomplished:

- ☐ Archery
- ☐ Biking
- ☐ Birding
- ☐ Boating
- ☐ Camping
- ☐ Caving
- ☐ Geocaching
- ☐ Fishing
- ☐ Hiking
- ☐ Horseback Riding
- ☐ Hunting
- ☐ Off-Roading
- ☐ Paddle Boarding
- ☐ Photography
- ☐ Picnicking
- ☐ Rock Climbing
- ☐ Shooting Range
- ☐ Snowshoeing
- ☐ Stargazing
- ☐ Swimming
- ☐ Tennis
- ☐ Walking
- ☐ Wildlife Watching
- ☐ _____
- ☐ _____
- ☐ _____
- ☐ _____
- ☐ _____

Traveled by:

☐ ☐ ☐ ☐ ☐ ☐ ☐ ☐ ☐ ☐ ☐ ☐

Add your favorite ticket stub, postcard, photo, stamp or drawing here

NOT ALL THOSE WHO WANDER ARE LOST

Queen Wilhelmina State Park

Address: 3877 Highway 88 West | Mena, AR 71953

Website: https://www.arkansasstateparks.com/parks/queen-wilhelmina-state-park

Phone: 479-394-2863

Email: queen.gen@arkansas.gov

Established: 1957

Size: 460 acres (190 ha)

Star Rating
☆☆☆☆☆

What souvenir did you bring home?... _____

My favorite thing about this place is... _____

_____

Why I went ... _____

Who I went with ... _____

When I went ... _____

_____

What I did... _____

What I saw... _____

_____

What I learned... _____

_____

An unforgettable moment... _____

_____

A laughable moment... _____

_____

A surprising moment... _____

_____

An unforeseeable moment... _____

_____

My List

- ☐ _____
- ☐ _____
- ☐ _____
- ☐ _____
- ☐ _____
- ☐ _____
- ☐ _____
- ☐ _____
- ☐ _____
- ☐ _____
- ☐ _____

 Snapped a selfie | Location... _____

 Took a park sign selfie? - Y | N   The weather was ...

- ☐ Trip Plan Completed
- ☐ Day Trip   ☐ Overnight Stay

Reservations required: ☐y ☐n

Date reservations made: _____

Refund Policy: ☐y ☐n Site/Room #: ___

Confirmation #: _____

Miles to travel: _____

Time traveling: _____

Dog friendly?: ☐y ☐n

PLACES WE DISCOVERED ALONG THE WAY

PLACES TO STOP AND SEE ALONG THE WAY

Would you go again?: ☐y ☐n   Open all year?: ☐y ☐n

Activities Accomplished:

- ☐ Archery
- ☐ Biking
- ☐ Birding
- ☐ Boating
- ☐ Camping
- ☐ Caving
- ☐ Geocaching
- ☐ Fishing
- ☐ Hiking
- ☐ Horseback Riding
- ☐ Hunting
- ☐ Off-Roading
- ☐ Paddle Boarding
- ☐ Photography
- ☐ Picnicking
- ☐ Rock Climbing
- ☐ Shooting Range
- ☐ Snowshoeing
- ☐ Stargazing
- ☐ Swimming
- ☐ Tennis
- ☐ Walking
- ☐ Wildlife Watching
- ☐ _____
- ☐ _____
- ☐ _____
- ☐ _____
- ☐ _____

Traveled by:

☐ ☐ ☐ ☐ ☐ ☐ ☐ ☐ ☐ ☐ ☐ ☐

Add your favorite ticket stub, postcard, photo, stamp or drawing here

LET NEW ADVENTURES
≫ BEGIN →

SOUTH ARKANSAS ARBORETUM

Address: 1506 Mt Holly Rd | El Dorado, AR 71730

Website: https://www.arkansasstateparks.com/parks/south-arkansas-arboretum

Phone: (888) 287-2757

Established: 1991

Email: museumnaturalresources@arkansas.com

Size: 13 acres (5.3 ha)

What souvenir did you bring home?... _____

My favorite thing about this place is... _____

Star Rating
☆☆☆☆☆

Why I went ... _____

Who I went with ... _____

When I went ... _____

What I did... _____

What I saw... _____

What I learned... _____

An unforgettable moment... _____

A laughable moment... _____

A surprising moment... _____

An unforeseeable moment... _____

My List
- ☐ _____
- ☐ _____
- ☐ _____
- ☐ _____
- ☐ _____
- ☐ _____
- ☐ _____
- ☐ _____
- ☐ _____
- ☐ _____
- ☐ _____
- ☐ _____

Snapped a selfie | Location... _____

Took a park sign selfie? - Y | N

The weather was ...

☐ Trip Plan Completed

☐ Day Trip   ☐ Overnight Stay

Reservations required: ☐y ☐n

Date reservations made: _____

Refund Policy: ☐y ☐n Site/Room #: _____

Confirmation #: _____

Miles to travel: _____

Time traveling: _____

Dog friendly?: ☐y ☐n

_____

PLACES WE DISCOVERED ALONG THE WAY

_____
_____
_____

PLACES TO STOP AND SEE ALONG THE WAY

_____
_____
_____

Would you go again?: ☐y ☐n   Open all year?: ☐y ☐n

Activities Accomplished:

☐ Archery
☐ Biking
☐ Birding
☐ Boating
☐ Camping
☐ Caving
☐ Geocaching

☐ Fishing
☐ Hiking
☐ Horseback Riding
☐ Hunting
☐ Off-Roading
☐ Paddle Boarding
☐ Photography

☐ Picnicking
☐ Rock Climbing
☐ Shooting Range
☐ Snowshoeing
☐ Stargazing
☐ Swimming
☐ Tennis

☐ Walking
☐ Wildlife Watching
☐ _____
☐ _____
☐ _____
☐ _____
☐ _____

Traveled by:

☐ ☐ ☐ ☐ ☐ ☐ ☐ ☐ ☐ ☐ ☐ ☐

Add your favorite ticket stub, postcard, photo, stamp or drawing here

Toltec Mounds Archeological State Park

Address: 490 Toltec Mounds Road | Scott, AR 72142

Website: https://www.arkansasstateparks.com/parks/toltec-mounds-archeological-state-park

Phone: 501-961-9442

Email: toltecmounds@arkansas.com

Established: 1975

Size: 185 acres (75 ha)

Star Rating
☆☆☆☆☆

What souvenir did you bring home?...

My favorite thing about this place is...

Why I went ...

Who I went with ...

When I went ...

What I did...

What I saw...

What I learned...

An unforgettable moment...

A laughable moment...

A surprising moment...

An unforeseeable moment...

Snapped a selfie | Location...

Took a park sign selfie? - Y | N

The weather was ...

My List

- ☐
- ☐
- ☐
- ☐
- ☐
- ☐
- ☐
- ☐
- ☐
- ☐
- ☐
- ☐

☐ Trip Plan Completed

☐ Day Trip   ☐ Overnight Stay

Reservations required: ☐ y ☐ n

Date reservations made: _____

Refund Policy: ☐ y ☐ n Site/Room #: _____

Confirmation #: _____

Miles to travel: _____

Time traveling: _____

Dog friendly?: ☐ y ☐ n

_____

PLACES WE DISCOVERED ALONG THE WAY

_____

PLACES TO STOP AND SEE ALONG THE WAY

_____

Would you go again?: ☐ y ☐ n   Open all year?: ☐ y ☐ n

Activities Accomplished:

☐ Archery
☐ Biking
☐ Birding
☐ Boating
☐ Camping
☐ Caving
☐ Geocaching

☐ Fishing
☐ Hiking
☐ Horseback Riding
☐ Hunting
☐ Off-Roading
☐ Paddle Boarding
☐ Photography

☐ Picnicking
☐ Rock Climbing
☐ Shooting Range
☐ Snowshoeing
☐ Stargazing
☐ Swimming
☐ Tennis

☐ Walking
☐ Wildlife Watching
☐ _____
☐ _____
☐ _____
☐ _____
☐ _____

Traveled by:

☐ ☐ ☐ ☐ ☐ ☐ ☐ ☐ ☐ ☐ ☐ ☐

Add your favorite ticket stub, postcard, photo, stamp or drawing here

LET NEW ADVENTURES
» BEGIN →

Village Creek State Park

Address: 201 County Road 754 | Wynne, AR 72396

Website: https://www.arkansasstateparks.com/parks/village-creek-state-park

Phone: 870-238-9406

Email: villagecreek@arkansas.com

Established: 1972

Size: 6,909 acres (2,796 ha)

Star Rating
☆☆☆☆☆

What souvenir did you bring home?...

My favorite thing about this place is...

Why I went ...

Who I went with ...

When I went ...

What I did...

What I saw...

What I learned...

An unforgettable moment...

A laughable moment...

A surprising moment...

An unforeseeable moment...

Snapped a selfie | Location...

Took a park sign selfie? - Y | N

The weather was ...

My List

- ☐
- ☐
- ☐
- ☐
- ☐
- ☐
- ☐
- ☐
- ☐
- ☐
- ☐

PLAN YOUR TRIP:

DESTINATION INFORMATION:

☐ Trip Plan Completed

☐ Day Trip   ☐ Overnight Stay

Reservations required: ☐y ☐n

Date reservations made: _____

Refund Policy: ☐y ☐n   Site/Room #: _____

Confirmation #: _____

Miles to travel: _____

Time traveling: _____

Dog friendly?: ☐y ☐n

PLACES WE DISCOVERED ALONG THE WAY

PLACES TO STOP AND SEE ALONG THE WAY

Would you go again?: ☐y ☐n   Open all year?: ☐y ☐n

Activities Accomplished:

☐ Archery
☐ Biking
☐ Birding
☐ Boating
☐ Camping
☐ Caving
☐ Geocaching

☐ Fishing
☐ Hiking
☐ Horseback Riding
☐ Hunting
☐ Off-Roading
☐ Paddle Boarding
☐ Photography

☐ Picnicking
☐ Rock Climbing
☐ Shooting Range
☐ Snowshoeing
☐ Stargazing
☐ Swimming
☐ Tennis

☐ Walking
☐ Wildlife Watching
☐ _____
☐ _____
☐ _____
☐ _____
☐ _____

Traveled by:

☐ ☐ ☐ ☐ ☐ ☐ ☐ ☐ ☐ ☐ ☐ ☐

Add your favorite ticket stub, postcard, photo, stamp or drawing here

NOT ALL THOSE WHO WANDER ARE LOST

White Oak Lake State Park

Address: 563 Hwy. 387 | Bluff City, AR 71722

Website: https://www.arkansasstateparks.com/parks/white-oak-lake-state-park

Phone: 870-685-2748

Email: whiteoaklake@arkansas.com

Established: 1961

Size: 725 acres (293 ha)

Star Rating
☆☆☆☆☆

What souvenir did you bring home?...

My favorite thing about this place is...

Why I went ...

Who I went with ...

When I went ...

What I did...

What I saw...

What I learned...

An unforgettable moment...

A laughable moment...

A surprising moment...

An unforeseeable moment...

My List

- [ ]
- [ ]
- [ ]
- [ ]
- [ ]
- [ ]
- [ ]
- [ ]
- [ ]
- [ ]
- [ ]
- [ ]

Snapped a selfie | Location...

Took a park sign selfie? - Y | N

The weather was ...

PLAN YOUR TRIP:

DESTINATION INFORMATION:

☐ Trip Plan Completed

☐ Day Trip ☐ Overnight Stay

Reservations required: ☐y ☐n

Date reservations made: _____

Refund Policy: ☐y ☐n Site/Room #: _____

Confirmation #: _____

Miles to travel: _____

Time traveling: _____

Dog friendly?: ☐y ☐n

PLACES WE DISCOVERED ALONG THE WAY

PLACES TO STOP AND SEE ALONG THE WAY

Would you go again?: ☐y ☐n   Open all year?: ☐y ☐n

Activities Accomplished:

☐ Archery
☐ Biking
☐ Birding
☐ Boating
☐ Camping
☐ Caving
☐ Geocaching

☐ Fishing
☐ Hiking
☐ Horseback Riding
☐ Hunting
☐ Off-Roading
☐ Paddle Boarding
☐ Photography

☐ Picnicking
☐ Rock Climbing
☐ Shooting Range
☐ Snowshoeing
☐ Stargazing
☐ Swimming
☐ Tennis

☐ Walking
☐ Wildlife Watching
☐ _____
☐ _____
☐ _____
☐ _____
☐ _____

Traveled by:

☐ ☐ ☐ ☐ ☐ ☐ ☐ ☐ ☐ ☐ ☐ ☐

Add your favorite ticket stub, postcard, photo, stamp or drawing here

LET NEW ADVENTURES
≫ BEGIN →

Withrow Springs State Park

Address: 33424 Spur 23 | Huntsville, AR 72740

Website: https://www.arkansasstateparks.com/parks/withrow-springs-state-park

Phone: 479-559-2593

Email: withrowsprings@arkansas.com

Established: 1962

Size: 786 acres (318 ha)

Star Rating
☆☆☆☆☆

What souvenir did you bring home?...

My favorite thing about this place is...

Why I went ...

Who I went with ...

When I went ...

What I did...

What I saw...

What I learned...

An unforgettable moment...

A laughable moment...

A surprising moment...

An unforeseeable moment...

My List

- [ ]
- [ ]
- [ ]
- [ ]
- [ ]
- [ ]
- [ ]
- [ ]
- [ ]
- [ ]
- [ ]

 Snapped a selfie | Location...

 Took a park sign selfie? - Y | N

The weather was ...

PLAN YOUR TRIP:

☐ Trip Plan Completed

☐ Day Trip   ☐ Overnight Stay

Reservations required: ☐y ☐n

Date reservations made: _____

Refund Policy: ☐y ☐n Site/Room #: _____

Confirmation #: _____

Miles to travel: _____

Time traveling: _____

Dog friendly?: ☐y ☐n

Activities Accomplished:

☐ Archery
☐ Biking
☐ Birding
☐ Boating
☐ Camping
☐ Caving
☐ Geocaching

☐ Fishing
☐ Hiking
☐ Horseback Riding
☐ Hunting
☐ Off-Roading
☐ Paddle Boarding
☐ Photography

☐ Picnicking
☐ Rock Climbing
☐ Shooting Range
☐ Snowshoeing
☐ Stargazing
☐ Swimming
☐ Tennis

☐ Walking
☐ Wildlife Watching
☐ _____
☐ _____
☐ _____
☐ _____
☐ _____

Traveled by:

☐ ☐ ☐ ☐ ☐ ☐ ☐ ☐ ☐ ☐ ☐ ☐

DESTINATION INFORMATION:

_____
_____

PLACES WE DISCOVERED ALONG THE WAY

_____
_____

PLACES TO STOP AND SEE ALONG THE WAY

_____
_____

Would you go again?: ☐y ☐n   Open all year?: ☐y ☐n

Add your favorite ticket stub, postcard, photo, stamp or drawing here

N
NOT ALL THOSE WHO
W E
WANDER ARE LOST
S

Woolly Hollow State Park

Address: 82 Woolly Hollow Road | Greenbrier, AR 72058

Website: https://www.arkansasstateparks.com/parks/woolly-hollow-state-park

Phone: 501-679-2098

Email: woollyhollow@arkansas.com

Established: 1973

Size: 370 acres (150 ha)

Star Rating
☆☆☆☆☆

What souvenir did you bring home?...

My favorite thing about this place is...

Why I went ...

Who I went with ...

When I went ...

What I did...

What I saw...

What I learned...

An unforgettable moment...

A laughable moment...

A surprising moment...

An unforeseeable moment...

My List

- [ ]
- [ ]
- [ ]
- [ ]
- [ ]
- [ ]
- [ ]
- [ ]
- [ ]
- [ ]
- [ ]

Snapped a selfie | Location...

Took a park sign selfie? - Y | N

The weather was ...

PLAN YOUR TRIP:

- [ ] Trip Plan Completed
- [ ] Day Trip   [ ] Overnight Stay

Reservations required: [ ] y [ ] n

Date reservations made: _____

Refund Policy: [ ] y [ ] n Site/Room #: _____

Confirmation #: _____

Miles to travel: _____

Time traveling: _____

Dog friendly?: [ ] y [ ] n

Activities Accomplished:

- [ ] Archery
- [ ] Biking
- [ ] Birding
- [ ] Boating
- [ ] Camping
- [ ] Caving
- [ ] Geocaching

- [ ] Fishing
- [ ] Hiking
- [ ] Horseback Riding
- [ ] Hunting
- [ ] Off-Roading
- [ ] Paddle Boarding
- [ ] Photography

- [ ] Picnicking
- [ ] Rock Climbing
- [ ] Shooting Range
- [ ] Snowshoeing
- [ ] Stargazing
- [ ] Swimming
- [ ] Tennis

- [ ] Walking
- [ ] Wildlife Watching
- [ ] _____
- [ ] _____
- [ ] _____
- [ ] _____
- [ ] _____

DESTINATION INFORMATION:

_____

PLACES WE DISCOVERED ALONG THE WAY

_____

_____

_____

PLACES TO STOP AND SEE ALONG THE WAY

_____

_____

Would you go again?: [ ] y [ ] n   Open all year?: [ ] y [ ] n

Traveled by:

[ ] [ ] [ ] [ ] [ ] [ ] [ ] [ ] [ ] [ ] [ ] [ ]

Add your favorite ticket stub, postcard, photo, stamp or drawing here

LET NEW ADVENTURES
>> BEGIN →

PICK YOUR OWN PLACE

What souvenir did you bring home?... _____

My favorite thing about this place is... _____

_____

Why I went ... _____
Who I went with ... _____
When I went ... _____

_____

What I did... _____
What I saw... _____

_____

What I learned... _____

_____

An unforgettable moment... _____

_____

A laughable moment... _____

_____

A surprising moment... _____

_____

An unforeseeable moment... _____

_____

My List

- ☐ _____
- ☐ _____
- ☐ _____
- ☐ _____
- ☐ _____
- ☐ _____
- ☐ _____
- ☐ _____
- ☐ _____
- ☐ _____
- ☐ _____

Snapped a selfie | Location... _____

Took a park sign selfie? - Y | N   The weather was ...

☐ Trip Plan Completed

☐ Day Trip   ☐ Overnight Stay

Reservations required: ☐ y ☐ n

Date reservations made: _____

Refund Policy: ☐ y ☐ n Site/Room #: _____

Confirmation #: _____

Miles to travel: _____

Time traveling: _____

Dog friendly?: ☐ y ☐ n

_____

PLACES WE DISCOVERED ALONG THE WAY

_____
_____

PLACES TO STOP AND SEE ALONG THE WAY

_____
_____

Would you go again?: ☐ y ☐ n   Open all year?: ☐ y ☐ n

Activities Accomplished:

☐ Archery
☐ Biking
☐ Birding
☐ Boating
☐ Camping
☐ Caving
☐ Geocaching

☐ Fishing
☐ Hiking
☐ Horseback Riding
☐ Hunting
☐ Off-Roading
☐ Paddle Boarding
☐ Photography

☐ Picnicking
☐ Rock Climbing
☐ Shooting Range
☐ Snowshoeing
☐ Stargazing
☐ Swimming
☐ Tennis

☐ Walking
☐ Wildlife Watching
☐ _____
☐ _____
☐ _____
☐ _____
☐ _____

Traveled by:

☐ ☐ ☐ ☐ ☐ ☐ ☐ ☐ ☐ ☐ ☐ ☐

Add your favorite ticket stub, postcard, photo, stamp or drawing here

N
NOT ALL THOSE WHO
W   E
WANDER ARE LOST
S

118

PICK YOUR OWN PLACE

What souvenir did you bring home?... _____

My favorite thing about this place is... _____

Why I went ... _____

Who I went with ... _____

When I went ... _____

What I did... _____

What I saw... _____

What I learned... _____

An unforgettable moment... _____

A laughable moment... _____

A surprising moment... _____

My List

- ☐ _____
- ☐ _____
- ☐ _____
- ☐ _____
- ☐ _____
- ☐ _____
- ☐ _____
- ☐ _____
- ☐ _____
- ☐ _____
- ☐ _____

An unforeseeable moment... _____

Snapped a selfie | Location... _____

Took a park sign selfie? - Y | N   The weather was ...

☐ Trip Plan Completed

☐ Day Trip   ☐ Overnight Stay

Reservations required: ☐y ☐n

Date reservations made: _____

Refund Policy: ☐y ☐n Site/Room #: _____

Confirmation #: _____

Miles to travel: _____

Time traveling: _____

Dog friendly?: ☐y ☐n

_____

PLACES WE DISCOVERED ALONG THE WAY

_____
_____

PLACES TO STOP AND SEE ALONG THE WAY

_____
_____

Would you go again?: ☐y ☐n   Open all year?: ☐y ☐n

Activities Accomplished:

☐ Archery
☐ Biking
☐ Birding
☐ Boating
☐ Camping
☐ Caving
☐ Geocaching

☐ Fishing
☐ Hiking
☐ Horseback Riding
☐ Hunting
☐ Off-Roading
☐ Paddle Boarding
☐ Photography

☐ Picnicking
☐ Rock Climbing
☐ Shooting Range
☐ Snowshoeing
☐ Stargazing
☐ Swimming
☐ Tennis

☐ Walking
☐ Wildlife Watching
☐ _____
☐ _____
☐ _____
☐ _____
☐ _____

Traveled by:

☐ ☐ ☐ ☐ ☐ ☐ ☐ ☐ ☐ ☐ ☐ ☐

Add your favorite ticket stub, postcard, photo, stamp or drawing here

LET NEW ADVENTURES
»› BEGIN →

PICK YOUR OWN PLACE

What souvenir did you bring home?... _____

☆☆☆☆☆

My favorite thing about this place is... _____

Why I went ... _____

Who I went with ... _____

When I went ... _____

What I did... _____

What I saw... _____

What I learned... _____

An unforgettable moment... _____

A laughable moment... _____

A surprising moment... _____

An unforeseeable moment... _____

My List

- ☐ _____
- ☐ _____
- ☐ _____
- ☐ _____
- ☐ _____
- ☐ _____
- ☐ _____
- ☐ _____
- ☐ _____
- ☐ _____
- ☐ _____

Snapped a selfie | Location... _____

Took a park sign selfie? - Y | N   The weather was ...

PLAN YOUR TRIP:

DESTINATION INFORMATION:

☐ Trip Plan Completed

☐ Day Trip ☐ Overnight Stay

Reservations required: ☐ y ☐ n

Date reservations made: _____

Refund Policy: ☐ y ☐ n Site/Room #: _____

Confirmation #: _____

Miles to travel: _____

Time traveling: _____

Dog friendly?: ☐ y ☐ n

PLACES WE DISCOVERED ALONG THE WAY

PLACES TO STOP AND SEE ALONG THE WAY

Would you go again?: ☐ y ☐ n   Open all year?: ☐ y ☐ n

Activities Accomplished:

☐ Archery
☐ Biking
☐ Birding
☐ Boating
☐ Camping
☐ Caving
☐ Geocaching

☐ Fishing
☐ Hiking
☐ Horseback Riding
☐ Hunting
☐ Off-Roading
☐ Paddle Boarding
☐ Photography

☐ Picnicking
☐ Rock Climbing
☐ Shooting Range
☐ Snowshoeing
☐ Stargazing
☐ Swimming
☐ Tennis

☐ Walking
☐ Wildlife Watching
☐ _____
☐ _____
☐ _____
☐ _____
☐ _____

Traveled by:

☐ ☐ ☐ ☐ ☐ ☐ ☐ ☐ ☐ ☐ ☐ ☐

Add your favorite ticket stub, postcard, photo, stamp or drawing here

NOT ALL THOSE WHO WANDER ARE LOST

N W E S

PICK YOUR OWN PLACE

What souvenir did you bring home?... _____

☆ ☆ ☆ ☆ ☆

My favorite thing about this place is... _____

_____

Why I went ... _____

Who I went with ... _____

When I went ... _____

_____

What I did... _____

What I saw... _____

My List

- [ ] _____
- [ ] _____
- [ ] _____

What I learned... _____

- [ ] _____
- [ ] _____

An unforgettable moment... _____

- [ ] _____
- [ ] _____

A laughable moment... _____

- [ ] _____
- [ ] _____

A surprising moment... _____

- [ ] _____
- [ ] _____

An unforeseeable moment... _____

_____

Snapped a selfie | Location... _____

Took a park sign selfie? - Y | N

The weather was ...

PLAN YOUR TRIP:

☐ Trip Plan Completed

☐ Day Trip ☐ Overnight Stay

Reservations required: ☐y ☐n

Date reservations made: _____

Refund Policy: ☐y ☐n Site/Room #: _____

Confirmation #: _____

Miles to travel: _____

Time traveling: _____

Dog friendly?: ☐y ☐n

Activities Accomplished:

☐ Archery
☐ Biking
☐ Birding
☐ Boating
☐ Camping
☐ Caving
☐ Geocaching

☐ Fishing
☐ Hiking
☐ Horseback Riding
☐ Hunting
☐ Off-Roading
☐ Paddle Boarding
☐ Photography

☐ Picnicking
☐ Rock Climbing
☐ Shooting Range
☐ Snowshoeing
☐ Stargazing
☐ Swimming
☐ Tennis

☐ Walking
☐ Wildlife Watching
☐ _____
☐ _____
☐ _____
☐ _____
☐ _____

Traveled by:

☐ ☐ ☐ ☐ ☐ ☐ ☐ ☐ ☐ ☐ ☐ ☐

DESTINATION INFORMATION:

_____

_____

PLACES WE DISCOVERED ALONG THE WAY

_____

_____

_____

PLACES TO STOP AND SEE ALONG THE WAY

_____

_____

Would you go again?: ☐y ☐n   Open all year?: ☐y ☐n

Add your favorite ticket stub, postcard, photo, stamp or drawing here

LET NEW ADVENTURES
»» BEGIN →

PICK YOUR OWN PLACE

What souvenir did you bring home?... _____

☆☆☆☆☆

My favorite thing about this place is... _____

_____

Why I went ... _____

Who I went with ... _____

When I went ... _____

What I did... _____

What I saw... _____

What I learned... _____

An unforgettable moment... _____

A laughable moment... _____

A surprising moment... _____

An unforeseeable moment... _____

My List

- ☐ _____
- ☐ _____
- ☐ _____
- ☐ _____
- ☐ _____
- ☐ _____
- ☐ _____
- ☐ _____
- ☐ _____
- ☐ _____
- ☐ _____

Snapped a selfie | Location... _____

Took a park sign selfie? - Y | N

The weather was ...

Notes:

Notes:

Notes:

Notes:

ADVENTURE

LIKE OUR BOOKS?
Check out some of these favorites in our National Parks Collections

National Parks Adventure Book
www.mynaturebookadventures.com

National Historic Sites Adventure Book
www.mynaturebookadventures.com